OnE
STORY
MANY VOICES

LAURIE ROBINSON SAMMONS
WITH CHRISTY IVIE

Printed in the United States of America

FULL CIRCLE PRESS

700 E. Redlands Blvd, Suite U #293
Redlands, CA 92373

Cataloging-in-Publication data for this book is available from the Library of Congress

978-1-7334494-9-6   010222

Copies of this book are available at special discounts for bulk purchases in the U.S. by schools, non-profit
organizations, and other government and private agencies. For more information, please contact the Special
Markets Department, Full Circle Press at 700 E. Redlands Blvd, Ste U #293, Redlands CA 92373 or at www.
fullcirclepress.org.

Cover design and layout by Laura Marie

No two crimes are identical. Each case is unique; each survivor is unique. Sexual crimes against children are frequently committed by a loved one, family member, or friend, but they can also be extremely violent and/or committed at the hands of one or many strangers. This book highlights several stories shared by survivors but does not encompass every sex crime committed against a child. The survivors' stories shared in this book are a snapshot in time and do not fully represent the entirety of each survivor. Because of the complexity of human behavior, dynamics will often be described on a continuum rather than as either/or categories. The material provided may not apply to every case or circumstance. The information and opinions shared are based primarily on the totality of the contributors' acquired knowledge, expertise, research, and cited resources. The contents' acceptance and application must be carefully evaluated by each person based on their agency/organizational policy and governing legislation. The use of mental health terms (e.g., impulsive, compulsive, pedophilia) is not meant to imply a psychiatric diagnosis.

Further, the opinions expressed by the primary author do not necessarily reflect the views of the co-author, publisher, and/or any of the contributors.

OnE
STORY
MANY VOICES

"At the center of the universe is a loving heart that continues to beat and that wants the best for every person. Anything we can do to help foster the intellect, spirit, and emotional growth of our fellow human beings, is our job. Those of us who have this particular vision must continue against all odds."

- Fred Rogers, Mr. Roger's Neighborhood

This book is dedicated to the brave survivors
who chose to SPEAK on behalf of those who still
fight to find their voice toward freedom.

don't settle for the smallness
they beat you into accepting

don't settle for the lies
they gaslit you into believing

lies like:
you're not good enough
your body is an object
you're crazy

but all the while
deep down inside
you knew; you've always known

they wanted to take your light
to snuff it out
because it enraged them

they wanted to use you up
consume you
because doing so made them feel stronger

but they couldn't
they simply couldn't

and now it's time
to rise from the ashes
to take hold of your destiny

one story
many voices
pushing back the darkness
shining our light
fighting for all to be free

in honor of all the survivors who participated in one story, many voices
either in this book or in their hearts
i dedicate this body of work to you
love to you all
- Elizabeth, Survivor featured in Chapter 1

CONTENTS

PREFACE 15

INTRODUCTION: LEARNED BEHAVIOR SPEAKS 17

PART ONE: THE STORIES

    CHAPTER ONE: HIDDEN IN PLAIN SIGHT – ELIZABETH SPEAKS.................25

    CHAPTER TWO: GASLIT – MEREDITH SPEAKS....................................45

    CHAPTER THREE: ISN'T HE YOUR BOYFRIEND? – ADDISON SPEAKS 51

    CHAPTER FOUR: FAMILY SECRETS – KRYSTEN SPEAKS................................59

    CHAPTER FIVE: ACCESSIBILITY AND OPPORTUNITY – JOLLY SPEAKS.......65

    CHAPTER SIX: A BROKEN SYSTEM – YVONNE SPEAKS.................................69

    CHAPTER SEVEN: EXPLOITED VULNERABILITIES – CHRISTA SPEAKS........ 81

PART TWO: THE STRATEGIES

    CHAPTER EIGHT: WRITING ON THE WALL..99

    CHAPTER NINE: WOLF IN SHEEP'S CLOTHING..111

    CHAPTER TEN: IF MY SUSPICION IS CORRECT 121

    CHAPTER ELEVEN: NAVIGATING UNCHARTED WATERS 137

    CHAPTER TWELVE: EMPLOYING CLINICAL SUPPORTS................................. 145

    CHAPTER THIRTEEN: ENVIRONMENTS OF HEALING 155

CONCLUSION 177

GRATITUDE 181

ABOUT THE AUTHORS.. 189

ABOUT THE CONTRIBUTORS 191

PREFACE

BY LAURIE ROBINSON SAMMONS AND CHRISTY IVIE

I first met Christy Ivie at an event launched by her foundation, Christy's Cause, which was established to build public awareness around sexual exploitation and raise funds to eradicate it. Due to Christy's own story of significant childhood trauma and abuse over nearly two decades, she has learned how to thrive and help others while managing her own mental health challenges. No one should ever have to experience what she and millions of others have survived. Our joint mission is to help end child sex trafficking and exploitation through resources such as this book.

No role is too small in helping a child navigate through their trauma in a safe, constructive way. It is often those nurturing encounters with a teacher, school leader, or another advocate who can instill a sense of worth within the child who has experienced trauma.

Christy shares, "When I reflect on my years in school, I fondly remember three of my teachers who genuinely cared for me, provided a structured and secure learning environment, and invested in me. I wish I could reconnect with them today and tell them that they made a huge difference in my life."

In some way, we hope that this book reminds all educators and advocates that the work they do matters tremendously. Though we address many of our strategies specifically to educators, the material speaks to the teacher in us all as advocates, professionals, and family members, whatever role we play. The strategies we recommend to educators, professionals, and family members in this book are intended to facilitate action plans for identifying, addressing, and ultimately ending child abuse and neglect. These strategies are outlined with the primary intention of creating a safe, nurturing space for children to feel supported and be vulnerable.

A few years ago, Harvard's Center on the Developing Child released a research study that noted, "No matter the source of hardship, the single most common factor for children who end up doing well is having the support of at least one stable and committed relationship with a parent, caregiver, or another adult" (Center on the Developing Child, 2015).

Christy further notes that "Educators not only have the primary role of providing daily sound instruction, but they also have become first responders in the classroom. In these uncertain times, it can often feel like the deck has been stacked against children, especially those living in unstable homes with little support and no one to provide a model for building healthy relationships." While it might be easy to adopt a cynical approach to complex issues such as childhood trauma, no act of kindness is too small, and the classroom might be the very place where a child can feel safe and thrive. The steps an educator can take toward fostering a safe and nurturing environment have the potential to provide hope for children suffering from trauma.

Christy further shares that, "Although the role of a first responder might not be an ideal position for teachers to be in, it does give them an excellent opportunity to be that one stable, committed, and supportive adult in a child's life. First responders need the appropriate tools to do their jobs effectively, and that is why we have invested over three years into this book project. We want to help equip you as you courageously become that stabilizing force in so many of your students' lives.

Together we can make a difference for those who desperately need our support and advocacy. We know these are complex issues to face, but we can say from personal experience that we are strong enough and our children are worth the fight!"

INTRODUCTION

LEARNED BEHAVIOR SPEAKS

> *"You are called to be set apart, not settle in. That means you need to be a culture changer, not changed by culture."*
> - JORDAN LEE DOOLEY

This book is, above all else, an invitation and a call to action. Will you sit with us for a while and listen to first-hand accounts, both harrowing and hopeful, of sexual exploitation, victimization, survival, and healing? Will you join us in the collective call to equip ourselves with the education, research, and strategies needed to truly advocate for and contribute to the healing of children and young adults who have survived the unimaginable and somehow come out on the other side? D. H. Lawrence once said that the "eye doesn't see what the mind does not know." This is why we believe that the voices of survivors are just as vital as every professional voice of advocacy, and we have carefully included both on the pages that follow.

The audience for this book is many – educators, survivors, parents and family members, law enforcement, medical personnel, counselors, and youth workers, to name a few. Since many child survivors of sexual exploitation spend more time in the classroom than they do with their parents, we specifically address the need for educators, counselors, and school nurses to be the eyes and ears when students exhibit red flags.

We hope this book is an urgent appeal to those called to action. As evidenced by the stories on the pages that follow, paralysis and repression often become the coping mechanisms for many survivors. A numb, robotic response often helps survivors deal with the trauma, and silence allows them the ability to cope – for a while. All of us who work with children are uniquely positioned to give voice to their struggles until they gain the skills and agency needed to fight for themselves.

If there was ever a time to step up as an advocate for children whose voices have been silenced, now is that time. An advocate is a professional, confidential, solutions-oriented truth-seeker of facts who protects a survivor's integrity and privacy at all costs. An advocate acts from a trauma-informed lens and helps build a support network around the survivor. An advocate is not a sensationalist or a storyteller who seeks to make a spectacle of the survivor, nor does an advocate seek to act as a knight in shining armor whose involvement in a survivor's recovery is more about personal gain than the survivor's support and healing.

The statistics around the sexual exploitation and commercial exploitation of children are staggering. In 2018, the U.S. had 3,960,823 referrals for child abuse and neglect. Of those, 2,402,827 were referred for investigation (U.S. Dept of Health & Human Services, 2020; Child Welfare League of America, 2020). Although those numbers represent all child abuse and neglect cases, according to the CDC, 1 in 4 girls and 1 in 13 boys experience sexual exploitation sometime in their childhood (Centers for Disease Control and Prevention, n.d.).

Children and adolescents who face sexual exploitation are far more vulnerable to commercial sexual exploitation (e.g., human trafficking, production of child abuse images). Worldwide, sex trafficking is a 150-billion-dollar industry involving 25 million victims. (Niethammer, 2020). Of all these victims, a quarter of them are children. And according to a 2019 report, 16.9 million reports were made that year related to child sexual abuse images, online enticement, sexortation, child sex trafficking, and child sex molestation (National Center for Missing & Exploited Children, 2019). As startling as these statistics may be, according to the Brennan Center for Justice, child sex crimes are dramatically underreported (Kimble, 2018). In other words, things are likely far worse than any of us can even quantify, and at no other time in history have we had a greater sense of urgency to stand in the gap for those who have been silenced and suppressed for far too long.

We all deserve the right to feel safe and secure under our roofs and in our family structure. And yet, as the statistics show, many children do not have this privilege, and the collateral damage of this often-complex trauma plays out within classrooms and on school playgrounds.

Part One of this book focuses on the first-hand narratives of survivors who range in age from five to eighteen at the onset of their abuse and represent a range of demographic variables to include families from those who are marginally financially stable to those born into extreme wealth. Most are from average income earning homes; however, one factor is predominantly visible in each of these stories – parental emotional neglect or lack of bonding in the early years of development, coupled with various forms of complex trauma. Out of respect for the survivors in our stories, the word "victim" is rarely used throughout the text. All the survivors have fought difficult battles for their personal freedom and have clawed through their hardship searching for wholeness. All have traveled a rough road filled with various degrees of extreme isolation, anxiety, lack of self-worth, and depression. Though these survivors may have found it difficult to speak their truth as children, they have done the work to heal from their childhood trauma and, as a result, are stepping forward to speak out as part of that healing journey. These survivors understand that while their journey toward healing was challenging, it allowed them to find the strength to empower and encourage others who have suffered through trauma.

As you read the following scenarios filled with multiple traumatic events, keep in mind that even though indicators like environment, culture, genetics, and mindset all have the potential to shape responses to stressors, individuals do have the power to redefine their responses to future challenges if they commit to practices that increase self-awareness and foster healthy coping strategies. Each of the contributing survivors has learned to rewrite negative narratives that held their minds captive, implemented strategies to navigate life successfully, and continued to invest in their mental health in positive and fulfilling ways. Their chains of silence have been broken, and they deserve our support as they speak their truth.

The hope is that by opening our hearts and minds to their stories, we will gain a more comprehensive understanding of survivors' complex and nuanced experiences in a way that better equips us to be advocates and allies in their healing.

As a trigger alert, we need to forewarn you that the nature of the content written in these chapters might be triggering. The graphic nature of their stories may require you to step away to process them and take a break before reading on. Some readers have been triggered or have experienced flashbacks as they step into the narratives, being reminded of their own traumatic experiences. It is okay to feel overwhelmed and need to step away. Do what you need to do to decompress before reading on. Breathe and be kind to yourself as you reflect upon the survivors' experiences and, in some cases, contextualize them within your own. Points to ponder are included at the end of the chapters as you read through the stories independently or with a class or group. Even if you're reading this book and completing the activities alone, we encourage you to seek out constructive dialogue around the topics covered with those in your community.

In Part Two, we take a deep dive into strategies, supports, and structures to help advocates use their professional roles and voices for good. All the book's contributors in Part Two have committed their professions to advocating for those trapped in sexual exploitation. Comprising the expertise of a teacher, a survivor, a curriculum writer, a nurse, a law enforcement officer, and a therapist, these chapters are full of research, and the voices of a wide variety of professionals in the field provide a comprehensive and diverse view of how educators can proactively be a part of the solution. You will also continue to meet some survivors whose experiences contextualize the research, practitioner voices, and high-yield strategies provided to help you better support the children and teenagers you work with. What you will learn in this section is that even though healing can take months, years, sometimes a lifetime, it is possible with the right support and resources. This section provides the hope and resilience that await the many survivors of sexual exploitation to reclaim a life full of purpose and freedom, illustrating how, out of the pain, the phoenix can rise.

Before we go on, we're going to take a minute to define some essential terms related to the topics covered in this book, as understanding terminology and how it's used is an important step in being an effective advocate. Child sexual abuse is the involvement of a child in sexual activities when the child has not yet reached the legal age of consent for sexual activities and/or participation in sexual activities is gained through means such as coercion, force, threats, abuse of a recognized position of trust, or abuse of a vulnerable situation, including mental or physical disability or situational dependence (Council of Europe Convention, 2012). Child sexual exploitation is defined as the sexual maltreatment of children, which consists of, but is not limited to, child sexual abuse, child sexual assault, child sexual abuse material, and early or forced marriage (Matar, 2006). Child sexual abuse material means any representation, "by whatever means, of a child engaged in real or simulated explicit sexual behavior or any depiction of the genitalia of a child for primarily sexual purposes" (United Nations Human Rights Office of the High Commissioner, 2000). While most legislation uses the term "child pornography," there has been a global movement toward using the term "child sexual abuse material" (CSAM) to more accurately reflect the fact that all sexualized material depicting or misrepresenting children qualifies as a form of child sexual abuse (European Parliament, 2015). Commercial child sexual exploitation refers to the maltreatment of children in forced sexual situations where some form of remuneration may occur – such as child prostitution, early or forced marriages, sale of children, trafficking children for sexual purposes, child pornography, and child sex performances. (Matar, 2006). Online grooming describes any deliberate actions taken by misusing the internet or other digital services to befriend a child under false pretenses to engage in sexual acts with that child either online or in-person (McGuire & Dowling, 2013).

Our intent in writing this book is to provide current best practices and awareness to a global audience with the research and voices of experts in mental and medical health, law, education, and curriculum. The power of the writing is in the balanced marriage of compelling story, science, expert voices, and practical strategies, tools, techniques, and resources to offer support and awareness to the reader. As Dr. Maya Angelou stated, when we know better, we do better. Educators have the opportunity to change lives through their knowledge and willingness to act on this knowledge in meaningful and proactive ways. Far more impacting than the grade level "intended" curriculum is the "hidden" curriculum, which capitalizes on the pillars of character. As both authors and advocates, we hope that you will experience a sense of urgency to explicitly act as a first responder, whatever your role may be. Through our individual and collective efforts, we can fulfill the primary mission of this work, which is "each one, reach one." So, sharpen your pencils, open your minds and hearts, and be prepared to do some hard work. Together, we can envision a safer future for all our children and work collectively to make this dream a reality.

PART 1
THE STORIES

CHAPTER ONE

HIDDEN IN PLAIN SIGHT

ELIZABETH SPEAKS

> *"When we keep our stories locked up inside of us, darkness wins. We must share what we've lived, what we've learned, and how we have become stronger through our experiences, in hopes that it helps others find their voice, too."*
> — LAURA GAGNON

It was in the late sixties, and for many, it was a time of communal living, free love, hard drugs, and an "anything goes" lifestyle. The story passed down from family members described a young, handsome soldier serving in the Marine Corps during the Vietnam War meeting an attractive, young woman one night at a club just off the Quantico USMC Military Base. They would eventually marry, and it was a marriage riddled with anger, violence, addiction, sexual abuse, infidelity, pain, and numerous family secrets. The unresolved wounds from this couple's abusive childhoods impacted their children, and their firstborn child is center stage in this story. Meet Elizabeth.

At first glance, Elizabeth appears quite approachable – tall and fashionably put-together, with compassionate eyes that immediately draw you to her warm, vivacious spirit. However, once she tells her personal story, a beautiful flowering steel magnolia emerges – one with a gentle exterior that has had to develop guts of steel as she recalls almost two decades of abuse.

Though the survivor is now middle-aged, Elizabeth retells snippets of her young life through the lens of a child who has cataloged her past like a box of old photo negatives. Inside the images' white paper borders, where the real story takes place, her memories are only snapshots frozen in time. She speaks softly and reflectively as she tries to fill in all the shadowy scenes, but the fragments only come in bits and pieces.

As you read her story, you will notice occasional shifts from one memory to the next that can, at times, feel disconnected. To Elizabeth, the incidents are connected, like the overlap of one continuous piece of yarn that has become so tangled it's hard to tell where it starts and where it ends.

• • • •

ELIZABETH SPEAKS
HOME LIFE

I don't recall much of my earliest years in the presence of my mother. To me, she fit the perfect mold of a classic hippy in her dress, erratic actions, and undependable lifestyle. I do not ever remember being lovingly held or hearing the words "I love you" from her lips. I do remember episodes of my mother running away and leaving my father to care for me. I loved him and depended on him to provide me with warmth and safety. She had a name, but "mom" did not fit her role in the life of abandonment I experienced. Weren't mothers supposed to be caretakers, protectors, and loving, nurturing advocates? I did not feel the woman who gave birth to me was any of these things.

When she returned to us after one of her absences, she spent days in bed, oblivious to our family's needs and disconnected from reality. It was not something that gave any sense of security to a little girl who needed refuge in the arms of an attentive mother.

Mother was often absent, so when my father worked, I would sometimes stay with my grandparents, who provided me with a healthy, nurturing routine and environment. Though I was in the care of my father most of the time, when he was heavily drinking, my grandmother became my safety net. I cherished her healthy presence and strong example amidst the inconsistent, unpredictable life at home.

One could reason that I would detest my father for drinking while caring for me, but it shows how the cycle of codependency works. I felt responsible for my father's happiness, and I was okay with taking on that role. It was not unusual to observe his violent temper. In fact, I became a tiny, five-year-old crisis negotiator to survive. I would calm him, maneuver quietly around him, rub his back, and comfort him. You see, I loved my dad, and I wanted my protector and hero to be okay. As a result, he had my undivided and loyal attention.

Leading up to my fifth birthday, significant change transpired as my mother returned home, seemed to make peace with my father, and baby two was born. What I remember most about this time of chaos was that my mother went entirely off the deep end. I could hear her crying as she stayed in her bed all day, totally non-functional. This left me solely in charge of caring for the baby. I wasn't big enough to lift a baby out of a crib, so I would reach my hands through the vertical slats to rub his little back, sing, and comfort him when he cried.

At this time, a personal rage toward my mother began to escalate as I felt responsible for caring for my brother but wasn't big enough to manage. I would race to her room screaming, throwing things at her, and telling her to "Stop crying and get up!" Her response always was the same: "Just wait until your father gets home, Elizabeth! You are going to be in big trouble!" And she was right.

After my mother's report of my inappropriate actions, my father would loosen his leather belt, fold it in half, and use it to beat me violently all over my body. He would grab my arm and swing his belt repeatedly as I ran in circles. As the leather hit me from my neck down my legs, I cried, "I love you, daddy! I'm so sorry. I promise I'll be good." It felt as if he would never stop, and my bloody welts proved it. He seemed to mentally disappear somewhere while taking out his pent-up rage on me. The cycle of abuse continued as I watched my mother blatantly neglect my brother; I would mouth off to her, she would tell my father, and I would get it with his belt.

Strangely, I blamed my mother for my father's extreme, hurtful actions toward me. I loved and protected my father, and I felt like she was manipulating him to carry out her devious commands. In my eyes, she was the villain, and I hated her for not caring for my brother and me.

Included in this time of significant change came the summer that the relationship with my father transitioned. I was happy to be a fully devoted daughter, but I couldn't process becoming his surrogate spouse. The sexual abuse started when I was only five, but that was just the beginning of hundreds of occasions that escalated and continued until I left home.

I recall watching numerous television episodes of "Happy Days" with my dad the summer he started sexually abusing me. The first incident took place late one warm evening. Dad had bought me a t-shirt I truly loved to wear, and it was one of the many things he offered as gifts to buy my silence. He proceeded to instruct me to take my shorts and panties off, and I argued with him about that, but in my attempt to negotiate, he got angry, so I gave in.

In the beginning, he did not penetrate my little body, but soon, on a particular day when the sun was setting, the sexual abuse progressed in severity. As things escalated, I looked out the window and drifted away. I don't know where I went. I just knew it was no longer safe to stay in my body. Whenever I could tell things were headed in this direction, I would try to talk him out of it. I would say, "Daddies don't do this with their little girls." His response was always, "Elizabeth, you are so special, and I love you so much. ALL daddies do this with their little girls." So, upon hearing this, I tried to understand, but I couldn't reconcile the sick feeling I had inside.

Even though I am an extreme germaphobe, I find it interesting that I have no recollection of blood or cleaning up after any of the assaults. I don't even remember the physical pain of him penetrating my little, preadolescent body. I learned how to completely detach whenever things became uncomfortable. It was as if I had been abducted to an alien ship and injected with some form of foreign anesthesia. All I knew was I didn't like what was happening and desperately wished I could escape, so I learned to escape in my own way. I became a quick problem solver and started pushing my dresser against the door so he couldn't get in my room during the night. My mother must have known he was pursuing me because she had to push the door open and move my dresser to wake me for school, but she never asked me any questions. As a teen, I tried locking my door, but his remedy was to remove my doorknobs.

From ages five to seven, he sexually assaulted me on numerous occasions. I was so completely ashamed and nauseated that I had to find out if these sexual activities occurred between other daddies and their daughters. I decided to talk to one of my school friends. As we were walking two-by-two to play at the park during a school outing, I quietly asked some probing questions, as careful as I could be, to find out the truth of what was going on behind the closed doors of her home. I was on my own personal fact-finding mission.

"Have you ever seen the white stuff coming out of a man's pee-pee?"

"Huh? What do you mean, Elizabeth? The stuff that comes out of my daddy's pee-pee is yellow."

After that embarrassing moment of disclosure, I knew that not all daddies did what he was doing to me, so I became even more paralyzed and trapped and felt further alienated from the other girls in my school.

My mother had always been one to distrust. I recall hook-and-eye locks outside my brother and my bedroom doors that confined us in our rooms. At an early age, I was told to go outside and play and "Don't come to the back door until dinner." So, I explored the outdoors, God's beautiful creation, as He spoke to me through fragrant flowers, buzzing bees, and other intriguing plants and animals. I felt at peace alone outside. Because I was locked out of the house all day with a lot of time on my hands, I would examine details like the dewdrops on the morning glories on our fence. These flowers would open so beautifully in the sun, and I'd greet them as I came out and say, "Good morning, Glories."

Despite loving being in nature all day long, there was also some significant abuse tied up in the mandate to stay outside. I had no access to the toilet, and I don't recall my mother giving me lunch. I was told to drink out of the water hose in the backyard.

But I adjusted and made the best of it. I loved burrowing a path under the honeysuckle vines draped over my fence where I could cool off and talk to my imaginary friend. I would pull off the blossoms, pick the stems out, and snack on the nectar. I would talk to the birds and bees, make up creative games, and construct the most impressive mud pies.

Among the most peaceful, happy times as a little girl amidst all the darkness came when laying on the lawn as long as I could and watching the clouds go by. When I felt lonely, I found solace in being close to God in nature. The sights and sounds were spectacular; the birds, flowering crepe myrtle, and cicada skeletons fascinated me. I was in love with God's flourishing creation, which brought me endless hours of escape.

One day, while playing outside, I really wanted to get a drink from the kitchen. My mother wasn't home, so I thought it was safe to come inside. As I went around the corner of the kitchen, I was abruptly confronted with the barrel of my father's cocked pistol. All I could see was a blur of steel. After my eyes focused, I looked down his arm and into his eyes to find nobody was home. That glazed, empty stare was more frightening than his gun in my face. I knew that look meant trouble. Without moving a muscle, I instinctually said in a very calm voice, "Daddy, it's me. It's Elizabeth. You're okay. Put the gun down."

I was the only one in my house who could calm my father. I had seen this empty crazed stare many times, and I knew I had to get him to snap back, or he was going to blow my head off. I had known pressures were compounding at his job, and he seemed more on edge than usual, which escalated the situation. I didn't breathe until I saw his finger come off the trigger as he lowered his gun. I knew at that moment I had dodged a bullet. Literally. I also knew he'd yell at me to make this situation my fault, but my young mind completely understood. I was actually relieved when he started screaming at me because that was far better than knowing he wasn't mentally present while holding a loaded gun.

Spit flew in my face as he yelled, "When you enter this house, you better announce yourself! You scream, 'It's Elizabeth, I'm coming in!'"

"Yes sir, yes sir," I responded.

To this day, I still announce myself when I enter my house. It's events like that that are woven into the core of who we are for the rest of our lives. I used to think, "If I just knew the rules, and they wouldn't change all the time, I could be better at this." That's the psychological part that can drive you crazy. Because you'll never know the rules, and they will always change! Life trudged on robotically, and I never told another soul about that day until I was engaged 11 long years after the incident happened.

I did not feel my mother ever once took my side when I needed her most during my formative years. To add insult to injury, on one occasion, she took me to the beauty shop and insisted the stylist chop off all my long curly locks, resulting in a humiliatingly short haircut. Then, in a moment of total detachment one night, I plucked out all my eyelashes – one by one – so now I really did appear to look like a freak! My mother reiterated that fact the following day when she saw me.

I began to have horrible recurring nightmares, three, to be exact. In one nightmare, I was in a large dark warehouse swinging on my swing set. I would hear a loud sound above as black coal began pouring from a shaft. The coal never stopped raining down on me as it covered my feet, knees, and chest. Before it covered my mouth, I would wake gasping for air. In the second nightmare, a man would come into my room at night and drain all the blood out of my body until I became completely flat like a piece of paper. The next day I would have to carry on with my responsibilities in this "flat" state with no one noticing. I tried my best to keep my flat paper body in my school desk. It was exhausting. In the third dream, I was always lying on my bed, paralyzed from my waist down as my father leaned over me and cut my legs into tiny squares. I don't know if you have ever seen those old-fashioned aluminum ice trays with the lever that you open and shut to break the ice into cubes, but it was as if my legs were cut into these tiny ice cube shapes. Then my father would hand me my red tights and say, "Put these on, so no one sees the blood." I would then have to figure out how to walk with my legs cut in these tiny cube shapes inside my tights. My nightmares were so awful that I dreaded going to sleep. I was always exhausted the next day from being tormented every night by a combination of being sexually abused and night terrors.

My mother couldn't stand the sight of me. I know this because she told me often, like when she would squeeze my mouth shut and dare me to cry after her numerous insults. My father would always come home uptight and start drinking. This was never good. I hated the charade my mother played in the evening. During the day, I had no food, but in the evening, I had to come inside, clean up, and play a role in her ludicrous script. Dinner would be on the table as soon as my father entered the door. I had to sit like a quiet little puppet and eat everything on my plate, no matter how many hours it took for me to choke every bite down. I know this doesn't sound too bad, especially after starving all day, but the combination of my father's temper that always flared at the dinner table and my mother cooking bizarre meals like liver and onions made swallowing more than I could bear. I was caught in this dichotomy of having no food or being forced to eat bizarre food with two crazed lunatics. Needless to say, my relationship with food growing up was always one that involved punishment. Looking back, I find it interesting that I watched my mother binge on food while she withheld food from me.

When I was 10, my dad was offered a job in another state which would take me far away from the one person who had become my only anchor of safety – my grandmother. At that time, I confided in her and told her that my daddy was touching my "private parts." I assumed she confronted him, and his reaction hammered another nail in my coffin. I felt responsible for his emotional well-being, and so when he sat me down to confront me about the position I had put him in, I held the weight of the world on my shoulders.

"Elizabeth, I know that you talked to your grandmother. If you tell anyone else, the police will come and take me to jail. When that happens, you will lose the house and the cars and be homeless. Are you prepared to do that to your mother and brother?"

That's all it took. I simply said, "No, Sir." End of story. I felt I had to sacrifice myself for their well-being. There was no question that he meant business. There was not much chit-chat with my father. Holding your tongue was the quickest way to get through most situations. Unfortunately, after that pointed conversation, the sexual abuse reached an all-time high. My father knew I was loyal, and he took full advantage of that as we settled into our new house several states away.

ELIZABETH'S POETRY

there are things
that have happened
that we simply
don't have
the vocabulary
to explain
because
there are things
people have done
to other people
that words
can't describe

My father was a very handsome man who took control of any room he entered. It was always uncomfortable going to eat at a restaurant with him because he often complained about the quality of the food, sending it back as many times as was required to get it to his standard of perfection. He would struggle to keep his composure while in public, but I can still see his clenched jaw and angry facial features when he was perturbed with the performance of others. I knew that I could bear the brunt of his anger when we got home if I didn't stay out of his way.

The level of shame and humiliation I carried was monumental. I was so incredibly trapped! I couldn't escape under any circumstance. My father threatened me in subtle ways to keep me silent. He was a brilliant strategist and could play mind games like a world chess champion. To make matters worse, the pistol he wore reiterated my constant fears. My childhood story time involved graphic details of each person he killed in the Vietnam War and how his buddies died. I was keenly aware that he would kill again if anyone got in his way.

One evening I heard a commotion outside my bedroom door. I peeked out to see what was going on, and to my horror, I saw my father violently throwing my dog repeatedly. I was overtaken with an urgency to help her, so I ran to my father's side and began to beg him to stop. The sound she was making was an awful one I had never heard any animal make before. Her eyes were terrified. I begged and begged, but my father turned with his jaw clenched and snarled at me to get back in my room. I knew I had to go, or he would violently turn on me. I shut my door that night and never saw my dog again. In the morning, I came out and asked my father where she was. He peered over his newspaper and calmly said, "She ran away last night. She won't be back." I knew in my heart he had killed her. I knew what he was capable of. I knew he would kill me, too, if one of his violent rages spun out of control. How could I ever trust a stranger with my secrets?

Though verbal sparring and threats of leaving were regular occurrences, divorce didn't seem appealing to my mother at the time. We lived a relatively comfortable lifestyle from all outside appearances, but we were not living the American dream behind closed doors. To me, it seemed my mother was more concerned with outer appearances than being an advocate for her two children. I battled a lot of rage when she finally gathered the nerve to leave after I went away to college. This particular exit was temporary, although she and my father eventually divorced.

• • • •

SCHOOL LIFE
KINDERGARTEN - FIRST GRADE RED FLAGS

Like any five-year-old child, I was excited to begin my first year of school. I attended an upscale, private school in the Southeast. The classroom was filled with color, creativity, and structure, and it was a welcomed diversion from the lonely life of seclusion I was living at home. My teacher was a kind man and a good teacher, and he created a safe environment where my creative mind could flourish. Unfortunately, things went from bad to worse when my "hero," my care-taking father, fell off his pedestal, and I lost my childhood innocence.

After the sexual abuse started, I began vomiting several times a day. Doctor visit after doctor visit and medications of various kinds didn't help. The medical staff administered shot, after shot, after shot without any sign of recovery. At one point, I was bedridden with a pot to throw up in, and my father would roll in the television to keep me company in the evenings. His brief moments of kindness were strong enough to silence the voice capable of exposing his secrets.

The doctor suggested the removal of my tonsils, although I was never diagnosed with tonsillitis. Though the vomiting eventually stopped, the abuse did not. The sickness manifested itself in so many ways, but no one saw the signs. The most challenging thing was not the beatings or the illness, but rather the heartbreak I carried that my beloved daddy, who was my hero and my protector, would do this to me. It was something I couldn't wrap my head around.

My grandmother cared for me before my tonsillectomy. To quell my anxiety, she prepared me for what to expect as I was prepped for surgery. I was instructed to take off my clothes and put on a hospital gown, and when I was told to remove my underwear, I hysterically exploded. I was terrified to be naked in a cold room with strangers. "Honey, this is a sterile environment, and we have to be germ-free. We need you to take your panties off during the surgery," said the nurse. I went ballistic! I knew all too well what slipping my underwear off meant, and I was not about to let the doctors or nurses touch me in the way my father did. As my advocate, my grandmother negotiated a plan with the medical staff to administer sedation before removing my underwear.

Another red flag that went undetected was my repeated absenteeism from school. I almost missed the entire year of kindergarten, but as I recall, nobody ever asked me why. Had there been conversations between my principal or school nurse and my parents about my absences, my thin body, or how emotionally detached I was?

After my tonsillectomy, I returned for the last stretch of my kindergarten year, where I saw the other children having fun without me. Despite my love for my teacher, I felt lonely and isolated. I was the odd one out on the playground, wilting in a sea of sadness. I was a devout rule follower and never got in trouble at school. But I did need breaks from the noise and commotion of the classroom, so finding a place of quiet refuge helped me cope. My teacher would find me balled up in the corner of a dark closet all by myself. This condition of cowering alone in a dark, enclosed space was a huge red flag that somehow went undetected. As I recall, nobody spoke up or referred me for counseling.

SECOND GRADE RED FLAGS

One day in second grade, I kissed a boy on the playground. I don't recall the details of the kiss, but I vividly remember what happened when my teacher marched me into the principal's office. My father had reiterated to me that this type of behavior was completely normal, so why would kissing a boy be inappropriate? My principal didn't encourage any open discussion that might have helped me feel safe to share why I was confused. Instead, I could feel her cold, stern eyes burning a hole right through me as she immediately accused me of watching too much television.

She interrogated me by asking what kind of shows I watched at home. When I told her that I had been watching "Get Smart," she shamed me for viewing inappropriate content. I was thoroughly humiliated and forbidden from watching the show again. She continued to elaborate on how "good girls" should act and that it was disgraceful that I had kissed a boy. I sunk deeper into my chair and wanted to disappear into the woodwork with embarrassment. I left that day deeply humiliated and terrified of my principal.

THIRD AND FOURTH GRADE RED FLAGS

Memorization was extremely difficult for me. Each week brought a new list of spelling words, and just the thought of the weekly lists overwhelmed me. I could never get my brain to remember the combination of letters or numbers. But I plugged away for hours at the dining room table, writing the list of words over and over and over, filling up the pages of my notebook. Afterward, my father would quiz me, and I always failed, so back to the drawing board I went, writing them again with hopes of success. It was an exhausting process because I could never remember the sequence of letters no matter how hard I practiced. Friday, the dreaded test day, always felt around the corner, and as the end of the week approached, my anxiety would escalate.

We moved the summer between my third and fourth-grade years. Once I arrived at my new school, I faced a whole new set of challenges. Not only had I moved away from the one consistent person in my life, my grandmother, but also the change of routines that came with attending a new school was debilitating to me. In addition to having difficulty with my spelling, I did not know my multiplication tables; memorization was not my strength.

At my new school, it was a policy to list the students who didn't know their times tables on a poster in the school's entry for everyone to see. Each day I had to enter the school through the front door and be publicly reminded of my failures. The humiliation was unbearable; I felt like I would vomit every time I saw that poster. I guess I managed to go into the administrator's office and recite them at some point, but since it was such a personal blow to my self-esteem, I can't remember any of it.

My grades rapidly declined after our move. The excuse my parents used was that the private school I had previously attended was behind academically, but I knew it was because the abuse had escalated, and I had no one to turn to for help. At this time, I begin biting my nails and chewing the skin around my cuticles uncontrollably.

FIFTH GRADE RED FLAGS

By this point, my problems were compounding at every turn. The sexual abuse was escalating, school was becoming increasingly difficult, and I couldn't focus in class. I was never a behavioral problem; I just couldn't retain information. It was like my mind was paralyzed; I simply couldn't think very well.

Math was becoming harder since one concept was built upon another. Because of my poor math foundation, instruction continued to be a blur, and at some point, I just checked out. My brain was not operating at the grade level required, so I was labeled "low-achieving." I felt so defeated that I simply stopped trying. As I slugged my way through the day, I knew corporal punishment would increase at home as my grades plummeted. It was a horrible cycle I could not escape, but I sucked it up because I didn't see what other choice I had.

To make matters worse, my breasts started developing before many of the other girls in my class. My thin, curvy body was becoming hard to hide, and I became the target of other girls in my class who teased me. It became another exhausting task to avoid the attention I was getting from the boys and, especially, my father.

MIDDLE SCHOOL RED FLAGS

When you don't want others to know the secrets you hide, lying becomes the only way to survive. Since I struggled academically, I lied to get extensions on assignments and retakes on retakes. I begged my teachers to give me second and third chances to avoid another beating at home for my poor grades, yet it was a no-win situation because I could not do the work successfully even with the extensions and retakes. I needed help, but I was never offered any academic assistance – no tutor, no after-school program, no assignment modifications. I never saw a guidance counselor, and no one ever asked me questions about my home life. I was just labeled a "poor student" as I retreated into my shell with yet another layer of failure and humiliation heaped on me.

Upon my grandmother's insistence, my father took me to the family doctor because I was so incredibly thin. Like a trained bodyguard, my father stayed glued to my side during my doctor exams to ensure the family secrets would not be shared. I discovered later that this behavior is quite normal in abusive relationships. The doctor looked at my fingernails at some point in the examination as if he suspected malnourishment. Then he looked at me and threw a questioning glance toward my dad. He did this several times. I was staring right into his eyes as if to say, "Please ask me some questions, PLEASE follow your gut instinct! Help me!"

I could tell the wheels in the doctor's head were spinning, and he was suspicious of something, but he must have been intimidated by my father's presence because he said nothing. Internally I begged him, "Please, just ask me a few questions. Ask my father to step out so I can talk to you." But his response was more than devastating: "Well, I recommend that you start eating a peanut butter sandwich and drinking a glass of milk with a little vanilla in it every night before you go to bed. That should do the trick." I sat on the examination table with that crinkly white paper underneath me as my heart dropped. I thought, "How am I going to swallow even one bite of that sandwich? That's the problem. I can't swallow! I can't stand the thought of putting one bite of food in my mouth before I go to bed! Do you realize what my father is doing to me in the middle of the night?" That was all it took. I was convinced no one cared. I left defeated. I stayed skinny. And no one asked me about my weight again.

At school, I began showing multiple signs of complex PTSD and OCD. I was very ritualistic about hygiene, routines, neatness, and organization. Social acceptance was critical in middle and high school, and I longed to be liked and accepted by classmates. I had a pair of fashionable Levi corduroy jeans in chocolate brown that fit me well. My classmates often complimented me on how I looked in them, so I decided to wear them every day. I would wash them at night, lay them out neatly, and wear them day after day. I wore them so much that a teacher finally asked my mother if I needed some school clothes. My mother made a joke to the teacher about my compulsive habits saying, "Elizabeth has a whole closet full of clothes that she is choosing not to wear!"

No one ever spoke up about my obsessive behaviors that became increasingly fastidious in and out of school. I was now obsessively biting my nails and chewing my cuticles until they bled. I usually had noticeable open wounds down to my first knuckle on each finger. When I was doing homework that required writing, it was never good enough, so I would rewrite it repeatedly until it was perfect. With my bloody fingers and malnourished body, I was organizing like a mad fool. Yet, no one inquired as to what was brewing behind my crazy, obsessive behaviors. I was emotionally numb, hypervigilant, frequently anxious, and had trouble focusing on my school assignments.

HIGH SCHOOL RED FLAGS

In high school, my lying skills skyrocketed. I learned to maneuver through many situations with the primary goal of avoiding my father's brutal beatings. By this time, he was punching me, grabbing my hair, and throwing me around the room violently. One morning he swung his briefcase and hit me in the head because I was running late. To this day, I have a neck injury from that incident. I learned to lie about anything and everything just to get out of trouble and get out of my house. Lying wasn't offensive in my mind; it was survival – end of story.

I repeatedly fainted for no apparent reason, which landed me back in the doctor's office. The blood tests revealed no medical explanation for my condition, and as usual, my dad monitored every minute of the exam. Wasn't his dominant presence enough to set off red flags of abuse to the medical staff? Never once was I questioned about what was going on at home. I never returned for medical care. It remains a huge mystery why I was so weak, but it appeared that my trauma was taking a toll on my body. If an Adverse Childhood Experience checklist (ACE) had been administered at this time (which you can read more about in Part 2 of this book), I would have scored a 9 out of 10, concluding high risk for abuse, neglect, and many adverse health conditions.

As my body continued to develop, I became more uncomfortable in my skin. Toward the end of my freshman year and into my sophomore year, one of my "friends" started relentlessly attacking me with snide comments about my tall, thin, developing frame. This continued with remarks made in front of my peers about my breasts, which later moved to false accusations about stuffing my bra. One time, my "friend" and her older boyfriend took me and another friend to a pornographic movie at a local drive-in theater. As another friend and I looked on from the backseat, my friend and her boyfriend proceeded to make out and later engage in sex without any discretion. That summer, while attending a camp together, my so-called "friend" managed to sneak in and take a picture of my naked body as I showered. I suspect she wanted proof that my breasts were real. Obviously, I was shocked and angry! She promised the picture would be destroyed, but little did I know the personal attacks would worsen when my nude photo circulated the school without my knowledge. When I discovered what was going on through another friend, I sat in my desk chair trying not to vomit and said to myself, "Put this out of your mind, Elizabeth!" I was trying to survive a regular diet of sexual assault at home, and now I was being victimized by my peers as well. At that point, I lost any hope of having a true friend. I had learned that not only could I not trust my parents, but my girlfriends were also untrustworthy. This resulted in me becoming even more emotionally disconnected and isolated. That fall, I was nearly date-raped by one of the football players, who I am sure had seen the photo. It seemed as if my vulnerability was increasing at every turn.

I am not sure how I managed to graduate from high school, but with graduation came my opportunity to leave home and be free from the steady diet of violence and sexual exploitation that had held me captive for so long. Luckily, I was accepted to a small college several states away, which helped me improve my math skills and take some basic classes to catch up. I was on my way to being free and in love with the thought that maybe one day I would experience "normal," whatever that meant.

• • • •

ELIZABETH TODAY

Upon meeting Elizabeth, one might not imagine that she survived 18 years of physical abuse and 13 years of sexual exploitation. She has fought hard to be open-hearted, loving, and kind. She is passionate about giving back to her community through philanthropic work. She has a loving family and supportive husband to whom she has been married for over three decades. She has woven spirituality and self-care into the core of her being. She often says, "I would have been institutionalized if not for God. He has been with me every step of my journey toward healing." Although she believes everyone is a work in progress and never achieves a state of wholeness this side of eternity, she has come exponentially far on her journey. Fear, panic, and paranoia no longer paralyze her, and she has learned to manage the aftermath of her trauma with grace and dignity. She fiercely believes that each of us can make a difference in the lives of children and that they deserve our advocacy.

Elizabeth is a champion for life. Her heart, soulful reflections amid chaos, and persistence in knowing there remains purpose and stability amidst seasons of change are inspiring. One of the primary reasons she is strong is not only her spiritual core but her insistence on rest and recovery through forgiveness, therapy, education, meditation, self-care, and mindful practices. She is genuinely an overcomer who offers hope to anyone who has traveled a similar path of physical, mental, emotional, and/or sexual abuse. Resilience and grace are her trademarks, and she is contributing in loving ways to make a difference in the lives of those with whom she comes into contact.

ELIZABETH'S POETRY

i'm learning to inhabit
my body again.
it's not easy
sometimes it can feel exhilarating,
so special it moves me to tears.
sometimes it feels terrifying,
so scary my whole body is clenched;
my toes tightly curled under.

although it's challenging,
i'm on a journey
to belong somewhere,
to be truly known,
to be truly accepted.

at some point i know
i will feel safe here
within this shell
i call me.

POINTS TO PONDER

1. Had you been on staff at one of Elizabeth's schools, how could you have collaborated with appropriate school staff to advocate and intervene on her behalf?

2. How did you see the survival skills Elizabeth adopted to cope with years of abuse play out in the classroom?

3. Children rarely disclose abuse. In Elizabeth's circumstance, what dynamics can you point to that would have made disclosing abuse almost impossible for her?

CHAPTER TWO

GASLIT

MEREDITH SPEAKS

> *"Heartache purged layers of baggage I didn't know I carried.*
> *Gifts hide under the layers of grief."*
>
> - SHAUNA L HOEY

Even one traumatic sexual assault has the potential to linger and eat away at the soul if left unaddressed. The second survivor had to finally face her past in order to repurpose her future. It took over 40 years for Meredith to confront her childhood trauma consciously, but hope springs eternal.

• • • •

MEREDITH SPEAKS

Growing up, I was a good girl who was very obedient, trying to please my parents. I had a sister a year older, a brother a year younger, and a mother who was overwhelmed by raising the three of us. I frequently was the one to volunteer to help my mother with chores. My mother was non-nurturing and often highly critical, making me feel unlovable and like a failure. In fact, my sister thought at one point that she was adopted because she couldn't believe that a blood parent would treat her children the way she and I were treated by our mother. When I was an adult, my mother finally admitted that she didn't enjoy us until adulthood.

My father, however, was more affectionate. He was also an alcoholic and was not much of a talker, which made life difficult in terms of communication. He was the general manager of our family business, and he served as president of the local hospital and country club. My parents' marriage was volatile with lots of arguments and door slamming at night, so our model for building strong future relationships was unhealthy.

My father had a coin box for his loose change in his dresser drawer that enticed me when I was a little girl. In second grade, I started taking a nickel out of it to buy a candy bar. Then it became a dime, then two dimes. One day, he caught me and told me to stop, which I did temporarily. Since the money was so easy to access, I continued to take the needed coins to feed my sweet tooth at the small establishment one block from home. Since the grocer knew my parents, he reported to my dad that I had become a regular customer in his store. That conversation raised a huge red flag, and my dad became enraged.

Days following, I was caught red-handed. That is when he spun into a rage and assaulted me by throwing me on the bed, pulling down his pants, and ejaculating into my mouth. I was eight years old and completely devastated. In my quiet, compliant way, I didn't go to school the very next day, a rare occurrence for someone who excelled academically. The event was so traumatic, and I never disclosed it to anyone due to the shame I carried. So, I pushed the memory into my subconscious until, at the age of 49, I finally began to deal with it.

• • • •

Meredith's assault was a one-time event that took a lifetime to process and address honestly. Unlike most sexual predators, there was no apparent act of grooming from her father. She did not have anyone to confide in, so she learned to survive within her private resources. She shared a room with her sister but never breathed a word. Meredith had been a thumb-sucker until this happened, but she started biting her nails and picking her cuticles after the violation.

During her elementary years, she completely erased the event from her memory. When her friends began dating in high school, she spent weekend evenings home alone. She did have a boyfriend away at prep school, but dates were few and far between. She shared that when they were together, they would make out, but she was always guarded, fearing that another assault might occur.

Meredith attended a woman's college for four years, where she felt safe and excelled academically. Her leadership ability was evident as she was elected vice president of the student government and ran the legislature. She seldom dated and was always on guard when in the company of men. While working as a teacher, she was proposed to twice, but she ran the other way as soon as they became severe.

Later she used her love of learning to excel in grad school at Stanford University, where she studied Physical Therapy. During those years, she infrequently dated, never feeling safe, until she met her husband-to-be in Southern California. Meredith shared that her husband was a kind, gentle, smart man with whom she felt safe. They were married for 20 years until their marriage began to unravel after they could not have children, and he refused to adopt.

Though she was a dynamo in the workplace, anger and sadness took control and made relationships difficult. Divorce shortly followed, and through the heartbreak of a dissolved relationship, therapy allowed her to adjust to the single life. In search of herself, Meredith attended individual and group therapy weekly and started going to special seminars. After 18 months of intense therapy, Meredith's memory of her father's assault was triggered during one of the sessions. It took several years of dealing with the painful recollection, which led to a season of deep depression. Finally, the therapist recommended one month of in-house treatment for survivors of incest. That month helped her deal with the anger and shame she had carried alone. Her mother and brother did participate in the family week and admitted that they believed Meredith's story, but her sister refused to believe that their father could have engaged in such a heinous act.

• • • •

MEREDITH SPEAKS AGAIN

After months of continued therapy, I finally came out the other side of the repressed memories on a pink cloud. I had been so angry with the world previously, and I didn't even know if I had any feelings. I was in a world of total numbness. But I knew I had to do the work to eliminate my accumulated bitterness over time.

MEREDITH TODAY

I no longer fear men, and I can enjoy their company now. Most importantly, I can also enjoy my own company without carrying shame or anger. This has been an intentional commitment to feel free, lovable, and beautiful. It took six years of very difficult work to get to this place, and it took me until I was in my 40s to finally reach out for intense, professional help. I am so lucky to have found the right professional help and have the financial resources to invest in quality therapy that has positively impacted my life. Many years after the incident, I did confront my father, and he didn't deny it. He simply said, "I don't remember the assault ever happening; I must have been drinking." He concluded by saying it was the sorriest thing he had ever done. I never spoke with him after that confrontation.

• • • •

Presently, Meredith supports multiple organizations dedicated to assisting children from abusive homes and lives with the freedom of knowing she put in the needed time in therapy to deal with years of accumulated anger and personal trauma. She is an avid golfer with a single-digit handicap. She is fully engaged in life and chooses to travel worldwide and enjoy each moment with intention.

POINTS TO PONDER

1. As advocates for children, how can we assist the "silent survivors" who have buried their trauma?

2. What did you notice about the family dynamics that may have contributed to Meredith's silence and withdrawal from telling anyone what happened to her?

3. Discuss possible damaging effects of unprocessed anger and rejection, especially in school-age children. Where did you notice these two elements in Meredith's early life?

CHAPTER THREE

ISN'T HE YOUR BOYFRIEND?

ADDISON SPEAKS

> *"Healing is never complete until we have been truly heard.*
> *May the universe send you someone who will sincerely care to listen."*
> - ANTHON ST. MAARTEN

Attitudes and belief systems about sexuality begin to form when children are as young as preschool age. These belief systems walk into the doors of every classroom across the country as parents send their children off to school. As unnerving as it may be to discuss the topic, sexual harassment and exploitation are happening with alarming frequency, and conversations around these acts are still often muted or ignored. What is sometimes passed off as bullying might, in some cases, be sexual harassment or even assault. Sexual assaults happen in school bathrooms, on school buses, in locker rooms, and on playgrounds. These crimes leave deep emotional and psychological scars that persist long beyond the act, showing up in survivors' social encounters, career aspirations, and everyday home and school life.

The increasing numbers reported has been one factor that has led to a plethora of safety and support systems developed to focus on prevention and survivor support, and numerous school systems across the U.S. are initiating curriculum to address sexual harassment and assault, sex trafficking, rape, incest, and red flag indicators of these crimes. However, sexual exploitation is a subject that many parents, teachers, and administrators still shy away from for various reasons, including the fear that delving into the issue will open up a can of worms that the system feels ill-equipped to address.

These fears often send messages to survivors that their experiences are too uncomfortable to address and that their safety and welfare are not a priority. When the school community indirectly reinforces these messages, it precludes many children and adolescent survivors from coming forward and reporting acts of sexual violence. Communities, families, and educators must find a way to remove the stigma of discussing sexual exploitation. As long as the stigma remains, predators will continue to have power over those they abuse. The facts remain that females between the ages of 16 to 19 are four times more likely to be sexually assaulted or raped than any other age group (U.S. Department of Justice, 1997). And it's important to remember that these numbers aren't just statistics, but real lives that are impacted and, in some cases, even destroyed in the aftermath of the assault or rape. Addison describes living with both the shame and nagging disruptions that occurred in her mind after she was sexually exploited.

• • • •

ADDISON SPEAKS

I grew up in a home that I would consider quite strict by most standards. When I reached my teen years, I gave my parents a run for their money, as I defied their rules and began to sneak out of the house. I also drank to the point of excess at local parties on weekends with friends in my small community. Everyone was doing it, and I didn't want to be left out. At the age of 16, I started dating a guy who raped me in a drunken episode that involved one of his friends, as well.

Like most high schools, homecoming events, proms, and graduations usually included alcohol consumption and heavy physical contact that often led to sexual intercourse. My friends and I made it a topic of conversation about how we might protect ourselves if "It" happened. It was graduation weekend in my 10th-grade year when I found myself locked in the back seat of my boyfriend's car between him and his friend. I started feeling very trapped, so I struggled to climb over the seat, unlock the door, and run out of the parked car. Even though the guys were high on weed, I was the one who had consumed the most alcohol, and they proceeded to have their way with me when we got inside the house. I actually heard them planning a scheme in the driveway, but I didn't think I would be the subject as they continued to take turns raping me. After being assaulted while under the influence, I passed out.

The following day, my friend's mother found me lying naked in the middle of the kitchen floor, vomiting and disoriented. If I didn't make it to work, I knew I might lose my job, so I slept a bit more, sobered up, and headed off to work. At this point in my life, I had already seen a counselor for bouts of anxiety. I had built a trusting relationship with my counselor, so I called him with details of the event, which spun me into a severe anxiety attack. He and his family were on a road trip out of state, but with immediate response, he called the local rape hotline and set up an appointment for me to be treated.

Monday morning came, and I was so ashamed of what had happened. Although I had bruises all over my body to prove there had been a fight, I still felt so guilty and blamed myself for everything. In addition to multiple bruises, I had deep bite marks all over my chest that have scarred my body years after the incident. I was taken into the police station, and the interrogation process began. The policeman recorded my story, and after we were all done, he turned the recorder off and pulled me to his face hatefully.

"Ok, Addison! We both know you are lying through your teeth! You just don't want to be pregnant with a Black man's kid."

I couldn't believe what I just heard. Both my sister and I had previously dated guys who were Black, so that fact had absolutely nothing to do with the rape. The cop continued to be so incredibly demeaning that I felt cornered, alone, and judged as a first-class liar.

• • • •

Addison was now in major panic mode. She felt guilty, ashamed, and now disrespected, unheard, and very shaken. Her mother took her to the Child Advocacy Center to get a rape kit and hopefully connect with someone who would understand and provide safety and support. To Addison, this experience felt like "standard protocol" rather than giving her the security and advocacy she so desperately needed.

After the rape, Addison's anxiety and depression began to take over, causing her to self-isolate. Her drinking escalated, and she also started to smoke pot. It wasn't long before the bottom began to fall out of her world entirely. Addison had been an accomplished student all of her academic life, and she had been highly involved in sports and other extracurricular activities, as well. But suddenly, she completely dropped away from social settings, quit the band and all further involvement in events at school, and spiraled into a deep depression. She had zero interest in anything. The more she checked out from engaging with others, the more her alcohol and drug use escalated.

Addison stopped all contact with her previous "boyfriend," and in fact, did all she could to avoid him for fear of repeated victimization or revenge. Eight months later, while driving her car, Addison spun into an immediate panic when she spotted her perpetrator, who greeted her in an oncoming car with his middle finger wagging wildly in the air.

Though Addison experienced daily flashbacks, her perpetrators, both minors, received no legal penalty or court repercussions after the rape, and she was left to suffer the consequences alone. In her book *Trauma Recovery*, Judith Lewis Herman's quote defines a common reaction in cases of rape, similar to what Addison experienced with her perpetrator: "In order to escape accountability for his crimes, the perpetrator does everything in his power to promote forgetting. If secrecy fails, the perpetrator attacks the credibility of his victim. If he cannot silence her, he tries to make sure no one listens" (Herman, 2015). Those circumstances became Addison's living reality — ridicule, bullying, and repeated lies spread across the school campus.

Addison went through two years of traumatic nightmares, flashbacks, and other symptoms of PTSD. Every time she saw a maroon car that resembled her ex-boyfriend's vehicle, her heart would race so rapidly that it felt like it was coming out of her chest.

One day, Addison was attending a school presentation on sexual exploitation when she became visibly triggered by some of the information provided on sexual crimes. All of a sudden, she was hyperventilating, loosening her jacket, and having what appeared to be a full-blown panic attack. She asked for permission to leave the presentation and go to her dad's classroom, which was an arrangement the school had made for Addison to go directly to either of her parents' classrooms when her anxiety attacks felt uncontrollable.

Though she was failing all of her classes, she somehow managed to complete her Junior year. She enrolled in a homebound program her senior year to graduate, which allowed her to access her assignments electronically and meet weekly with her instructors to discuss her progress.

Addison was fortunate enough to have strong support from her parents, who signed her up for regular trauma therapy sessions to help her begin healing. However, her family dynamics were affected immensely in the aftermath of her assault, and her family is still working slowly through this, each in their own way. Initially, she detested having two sets of parental eyes watching her every move after the incident occurred, although, with time, she came to better understand their need to protect her however they could. Most importantly, her suicidal thoughts are now gone, and she knows where to reach out for support during those times when she still needs it.

• • • •

ADDISON'S MOTHER SPEAKS

This is one of the most difficult things our family has ever faced. As a parent, you want the best for your children, but sometimes you just don't know how to handle all the complexities, especially in matters of abuse. It has been more difficult for my husband than for me. I'm afraid that if he had known all the details of the rape, he would have taken severe revenge. Ultimately, this scenario caused me to leave my job because I was working alongside the professionals who knew the details of the rape but failed to act on Addison's behalf. The community connections were far too tight in our small town, which affected the outcome of there never being any consequences for her perpetrators, which worked against my daughter tremendously. The reporting officers accused her of making this up and dropped the case. I was so angry with their lack of action since I believed wholeheartedly that Addison's experience was true.

One of the most anxious 24 hours of our lives was when I took Addison to the Health Department to be tested for sexually transmitted diseases (STDs). The test results came back positive, and our world temporarily came unglued. We cried and cried for hours, wondering what twists the future would take with these results hanging over Addison's life. The nurse presented many scenarios and requested a detailed sexual history so former sexual partners could be contacted for testing. Call it a motherly instinct, but something told me internally that the test was wrong. In desperation, I set up another exam at a nearby clinic to ensure the test results were accurate. Sure enough, as my daughter and I were talking in the lobby, the nurse called us in to inform us that the first assessment was incorrect. Addie was, in fact, HIV-negative.

ADDISON SPEAKS

My mother and I had talked about sex since the age of 14 when I requested birth control. I had always been a "daddy's girl," and this kind of conversation would never have taken place without significant opposition. Even though I always felt close to my dad, we strayed from one another during my teen years. Now that I am older, I find his role more like a friend than a parent. After all of this happened, he became very quiet and protective of me. What bothered me so much was that he wouldn't look at me. I carried so much guilt that I had let him down, but now our connection is stronger. Forgiveness has released the former tensions, but this has been a long, difficult process.

I have found myself to be more hypervigilant since all this took place. There are times I observe sketchy people watching others and following them around. Recently I was in Walmart and overheard a man trying to give a group of teenagers a ride home, and my inner filter took over. It was visible the students had been drinking, and I became so upset with what I heard, I called the police. My life has taken a turn, and I will do whatever I can so others can avoid situations similar to what I experienced when under the influence. I am on a continual journey for significance and purpose, and I won't stop until I reach it.

· · · ·

ADDISON TODAY

Though Addison chose not to go to the prom or other high school events during her senior year, she graduated with her class and is now successfully on track to complete a college degree in engineering. Though she still suffers from flashbacks and anxiety, she is on her way to recovery, living in a new community where she is building healthy systems of support. She is happily married to a man who supports her fully and provides her with safety and unconditional love.

POINTS TO PONDER

1. What are some healthy ways we can have age-appropriate conversations with our students and/or our children about safely navigating a sexually charged culture?

2. As educators, we are mandated reporters when a minor is a victim of a crime. After calling the appropriate child protective service and law enforcement, what additional referrals, like the National Center for Missing and Exploited Children (www.missingkids.org), can we provide to victims and their families?

CHAPTER FOUR

FAMILY SECRETS

KRYSTEN SPEAKS

> *"You cannot change what you will not confront."*
> - T.D. JAKES

The empirical data shows that sexual exploitation among children is on the rise. Nearly 70% of reported assaults occur with children 17 and younger (YWCA, 2017). According to a 2018 U.S. Department of Health and Human Services study, Child Protective Services (CPS) can substantiate or confirm allegations of child sexual abuse every nine minutes. In 2016 alone, CPS agents confirmed that 57,329 children had been victims of child sexual abuse (RAINN, n.d.). It is estimated that one in four girls and one in thirteen boys have experienced sexual abuse as children (Center for Disease Control and Prevention, 2021). A 2018 national study on sexual harassment and assault from Stop Street Harassment found that 57% and 42% of women and men respectively had reported some form of sexual harassment or sexual assault by the age of 17 (Stop Street Harassment, 2018). Ninety-five percent of children who are sexually exploited know their abuser personally, leaving only 5% pursued by strangers, which leads us to Krysten's story (Sanders, 2017).

• • • •

KRYSTEN SPEAKS

I grew up in a middle-class family with one younger sister, a mother who was a teacher, and a dad who worked in sales. I was well provided for and had many positive experiences as a child. My family placed a high value on being together, so my sister and I enjoyed weekend sleepovers at my grandparents' home. This was a regular activity we looked forward to, but at the age of seven, those events became a nightmare that chased me for years. This was when my younger sister and I became victims of sexual abuse at the hands of my step-grandfather.

There was far too much shame in telling anyone, but when a high-achieving student began a downward spiral of absenteeism and frequent illness, it was apparent that something was wrong. I was a once-happy child who became introverted and angry. Even after I was called in to see the school counselor, no one could figure out what was going on in my world, so I developed a layer of toughness to protect myself.

By age 10, I could not manage the abuse independently, so I finally confided in my parents. They immediately confronted my step-grandfather, and though he did admit to the abuse, my parents did not remove me from opportunities for him to continue the abusive contacts. The abuse escalated, and he became much more skilled at performing his acts behind closed doors, even when guests were present.

This abuse profoundly affected my confidence and self-worth. I became very fearful, ashamed, and condemned. To compensate for how I felt inside, I presented myself as a bold child who didn't care what anyone thought about me. As I aged, I began drinking to dull the pain and became highly promiscuous to receive the love I never felt as a child.

I still do not understand why I was forced to spend time with my abuser. My parents' response was always, "We don't want to talk about those things; it will bring shame to all of us. Just act normal, Krysten!" It took many years to come to terms with that answer and forgive my parents. I finally had the guts to confront my mother in the last days of her life, allowing us to heal emotionally and forgive.

• • • •

This story captures the devastation of a high-achieving fourth-grader who was sexually exploited, told the truth in hopes of being safeguarded, and then was expected to live as if nothing had happened. Krysten recalled the day vividly when she and her sister sat quietly on the sofa as her mother confronted their perpetrator on the front porch. The step-grandfather's first response was denial, and then came the response from her grandmother that stuck indelibly: "You little bitch! How could you do this to our family? You've destroyed us! Just look at what you have done!"

Krysten was silenced until years later, when she was able to unravel the trauma and begin healing through therapy. Krysten's mother did contact the school counselor, but after four short sessions, Krysten was dismissed from counseling for "acting out inappropriately." For Krysten, this was only one bit of evidence that proved the incompetence of the professional who was supposed to help her process the trauma. She decided that she would never allow an adult to hurt her in any way ever again, so she constructed a protective, indestructible shield. Krysten felt that her grandmother knew something was going on because when the step-grandfather was left alone with the girls, she was always expected to make a mandatory call that announced her return home. The step-grandfather did not want to be caught in the act.

Like with most predators, the assaults began with touching, kissing, and hugging before graduating to fondling his genitals, which later escalated to years of incest with both Krysten and her sister. One Thanksgiving with a house full of guests, Krysten was taken to the bedroom, forced on the bed behind a locked door, and assaulted. Desperately she wanted to scream but remembered the conversation about not disgracing the family, so she silenced her voice and felt completely trapped.

In middle school, Krysten pulled away from other girls and became a victim of bullying. In high school, she plunged herself into the party life and sex scene in the hopes of being popular, and, for a while, she enjoyed the status. With heightened guilt came years of suffering that produced a young, extremely perfection-driven woman who guarded herself through manipulation and control. In addition to PTSD and OCD came multiple health risks as she purged regularly and developed bulimia.

As a young adult, Krysten found release and control in fitness; however, it became an obsession, running seven days a week and teaching 8 to 12 aerobic classes in the same time frame. Eventually, the wear and tear on her body led to one neck and two back surgeries. Hospitalization was required to rest and recharge her over-taxed body and mind.

KRYSTEN TODAY

Krysten is dedicated to successfully turning the corner and choosing a healthy path for her future. At times, it feels like two steps forward and five steps back with the events of a divorce, distance from her abuser and certain family members, a renewed and healing spiritual journey, and the reality that she doesn't have to perform or be perfect to be loved. OCD and control issues continue to be struggles, but she has made significant progress forward. Her message is clear – without a regular therapy regimen and her faith, suicide could have become a reality. She now celebrates hope and a future in a second marriage to a faithful man who knows her story intimately and loves her unconditionally. She has a heart of passion for abused women and is dedicated to helping them find healing and a voice. As she has peeled back the painful layers of her past, it is visible that she is happier, healthier, resilient, and loved.

POINTS TO PONDER

1. What similarities are apparent between the trauma-induced responses of Meredith, Addison, and Krysten?

2. How can trauma and stress-related disorders in children present like behavioral issues at school?

3. As Krysten's life began spiraling out of control in the fourth grade, what changes did you notice in her ability to function as a high-achieving student and well-liked classmate?

CHAPTER FIVE
ACCESSIBILITY AND OPPORTUNITY
JOLLY SPEAKS

> *"Childhood trauma does not come in one single package."*
> - ASA DON BROWN

Every parent sending their children off to school wants the assurance of a safe and secure school environment. Without exception, educational settings should be places for children to bloom and grow in the most nurturing conditions. Although sexual predators make up a small percentage of educators, predatory human beings lurk in every profession. Shakeshaft and Sutton (2004) noted that since over 90 percent of the perpetrators are found within the immediate sphere of influence of a vulnerable child, we need to be aware of the following potential warning signs that may point to sexual misconduct.

Carol Shakeshaft, a professor at Virginia Commonwealth University who researched sexual misconduct by educators, reported warning signs of possible sexual misconduct that parents, students, and other educators should be aware of. For example, there may be obvious or inappropriate preferential treatment of a student, with excessive time spent in and out of the classroom or private spaces. We should be suspicious if an adult befriends a child's parent(s) by making frequent visits to their home or offering to perform favors like giving rides regularly to and from places. There is an additional cause for concern if an adult acts as the student's "confidante" and/or offers gifts, personal letters, makes inappropriate calls, or interacts with them on social media. At times, observing peers might pick up on flirtatious cues or off-color remarks directed toward a student that become "jokes" in the hallway or locker room ("Districts Should Appoint," 2006; Shakeshaft, 2004; Sutton, 2004).

These opportunistic predators often blend in and spend a lot of time around students, hanging out with them and going places they go. They tend to know a lot about students' personal lives and often work hard to be popular, which can lure potential victims into developing a false sense of trust (Frank, 2018).

Jolly's story reiterates the above-mentioned warning signs. The sexual assault she survived from a trusted and respected teacher temporarily interfered with her ability to flourish and grow as she should have been able to.

JOLLY SPEAKS

There are people you are immediately drawn to because they are adventurous, youthful, and fun to be around. Though this man was a coach and favorite teacher in our community, I knew him first and best as my parents' friend. We spent a lot of time with his family during the school week and on weekends. Coach was always the life of the party. Though he was animated in front of the classroom, he showed his stripes when he was partying. He was more of a friend than a teacher, but I enjoyed being around him, and all the popular kids felt the same way. He made me feel accepted, and he always commented how mature I was for my age during sleepovers with his daughter and son.

• • • •

Jolly fits her name. She is a focused, vivacious, and motivated young lady who lights up any room she enters. Whatever she commits to, she pursues with excellence, whether it be athletics, cheerleading, student government, community and church events, or academics. Since this is Jolly's natural-born personality, what would suddenly cause withdrawal and undiagnosed illness?

Jolly has always placed a high value on approval from peers, parents, community members, and teachers. While in elementary school, Jolly's parents divorced, which changed the family dynamics with Coach for a short time. As a single mother heavily invested in completing her nursing degree, Jolly's mom often dropped Jolly off with her best friend, Coach's wife. One weekend at a sleepover, Coach was watching television with all the kids.

Jolly recalls vividly Coach's words that night: "Jolly, this looks so gay that I am laying here next to my son in bed watching T.V. Why don't you come over here next to me?"

Jolly fell asleep and was awakened to Coach's hands in places they should not have been. Increasingly, as Jolly's mother dropped her off at Coach's home, she seemed reluctant and fearful to be alone in his presence. She exhibited recurring headaches, stomachaches, and periods of blacking out without notice. Even with the help of a medical doctor and a counselor, Jolly's parents did not get any answers for her drastically changed behavior.

One night while playing "Truth or Dare" at a classmate's sleepover, Jolly confided that Coach had been touching her inappropriately. She feared being found out and made her friend swear not to tell anyone, especially Jolly's mother. Naturally, her best friend informed her mother about Jolly's "secret" that led to the disclosure of repeated sexual assaults.

JOLLY TODAY

Because of the proactive stance taken by Jolly's mother and Jolly herself, numerous cheerleaders, athletes, and students came forward to tell similar stories to seal a conviction against Coach. Presently, the perpetrator is behind bars on multiple sexual assault charges, and the survivors tell their stories to others as they heal. Jolly's message to others is simple and strong: "Don't be afraid to tell your story. You MUST tell so that the assaults will stop!" She shares her story with others and stands strong as a successful student leader in her community.

POINTS TO PONDER

1. Predators look for ways to exploit potential victims. What vulnerabilities did Jolly exhibit at the time her sexual abuse began?

2. Just as there are no stereotypical victims, there are no stereotypical predators. What are some ways in which Coach does not fit the stereotypical portrayal of a child predator?

3. What evidence of resilience do you detect in Jolly's scenario that might contribute to her current life?

CHAPTER SIX

A BROKEN SYSTEM

YVONNE SPEAKS

> *"The thief comes only to steal, to kill, and to destroy; I have come that you might have life, and they might have it more abundantly."*
> - JOHN 10:10

As issues in our society grow more complex, so does the response of our children's welfare system. Why does the system we created to protect vulnerable children face so many challenges? Do we fully understand the system's intricacies and how it operates? Are we fully aware of the volume of cases of maltreated children in the United States?

The child welfare system is defined as a group of services designed to promote the well-being of children by ensuring safety, achieving permanency, and strengthening families. While the primary responsibility for child welfare services rests with the States, the Federal Government supports States through program funding and legislative initiatives (Child Welfare Information Gateway, 2020). Originally designed as a temporary resource for families in need dating back to the early 20th century, the child welfare system was never intended to serve the volume of families it does today (Gordon, 2011). Composed of public agencies, private entities, and community-based organizations that vary wildly from state to state, it is easy to recognize a lack of consistency and clarity within the system (Chibnall et al., 2003.) When you add policy that often has conflicting goals – child protection and family preservation – reconciliation between the two often fall in the hands of Child Protective Services (CPS), which are the state or local agencies responsible for screening reports of child abuse and neglect, deciding whether abuse or neglect has actually occurred, and then determining the appropriate response (Welch and Haskins, 2020).

It is no secret that a high workforce turnover rate exists in the child welfare field (Casey Family Programs, 2017). Casey Family Programs, the nation's largest operating foundation focused on safely reducing the need for foster care in the United States, published a report on how high staff turnover affects finding the best outcomes for America's vulnerable children. You can find this report in the resource section on our website (Casey Family Programs, 2017). The report goes on to say, "Investing in the child welfare workforce is an essential activity of any child welfare agency, because a well-trained, highly-skilled, well-resourced and appropriately deployed workforce is foundational to a child welfare agency's ability to achieve best outcomes for the vulnerable children, youth and families it serves" (Casey Family Programs, 2017).

When the numbers of children within the system are factored in, the situation escalates tremendously. In 2018, the U.S. had 3,960,823 total child abuse and neglect referrals. Of those, 2,402,827 were referred for investigation (U.S. Department of Health & Human Services, 2020; Child Welfare League of America, 2020). Of those, 677,529 children were victims of maltreatment (U.S. Department of Health & Human Services, 2020). Children served by the foster care system in 2018 numbered 687,345 (Child Welfare League of America, 2020).

The Children's Defense, an organization advocating for policies for a better future for our children, stated that, "Children in foster care are among the most vulnerable children in America" (Children's Defense Fund, 2021). The National Center for Missing and Exploited Children (NCMEC) reports, "Child welfare professionals play a critical role in preventing, intervening in, and providing a comprehensive service response to child victims of commercial sexual exploitation. Data and lived experience of survivors has revealed children in the care of social services are disproportionately vulnerable to commercial sexual exploitation. Perpetrators commonly target and recruit youth who have already experienced a disrupted home life and childhood sexual exploitation." You can access NCMEC's training resource, "Child Sex Trafficking in America: A Guide for Child Welfare Professionals," in the resource section available on this book's website.

How can these complex factors affect a maltreated child in America? As well-intended as our child welfare system is in protecting, advocating on behalf of, and placing maltreated children, the following story reveals this goal was not achieved for Yvonne. In fact, she was placed in a new foster home in her small community every year from age 5 to 18. For her, the child welfare system was broken and didn't protect her in the way it was intended.

• • • •

YVONNE SPEAKS

I was a good kid with an extremely unstable home, yet I have many fond childhood memories with my sister. Somewhere along the way, my parents were no longer good enough for each other, so they split. My mother was drinking a lot, and I'd see her with many other men, so my dad thought it was best for my sister and me to stay with him temporarily. I dreamed of a life where my father would come running, fix my scraped knee, and make it all better if I was hurt. I should have been able to look at my father and smile and receive a sweet kiss on my cheek, but instead, I received a look of lust in his eyes and sweat on his brows. This was the beginning of being removed from my home and placed in multiple foster homes that left a huge scar on my life.

My mother lived in a small shack with three rooms and an outhouse, and my sister and I did live with her for a short time when I was five. Although we had electricity, the shack was heated by a wood-burning stove. The outhouse had two holes in it, so both my sister and I could use it simultaneously, which we thought was cool. The adults were allowed to use toilet paper to clean themselves up, but my sister and I had to use newspapers. This was our life in the woods.

Most of the time, when I stayed with my mother, I ended up sitting in the backseat of the car with a can of Shasta and a bag of cheese curls for a snack. I realized before long it was mom's way of keeping us occupied while she and her boyfriend sat in the bar and got drunk. Then she would come out of the bar wasted, and a bunch of extra people would climb in the car as we drove home and the partying continued. My mom would be yelling from the front seat to kiss my "uncles." I hated their gross smells, and as soon as the car stopped, I would jump off the lap of a random stranger and run into my mother's room. My sister and I learned to hide food in the shed, eat berries from the trees, and sneak out when the parties got too wild so we could avoid the loud noise and craziness. We would come back inside to screaming, fighting, and couples touching each other inappropriately for young eyes to see.

At school, it seemed like everyone was related to each other. Everybody knew about it when bad things happened, so I never felt a sense of privacy. I don't ever remember feeling protected by any of the adults in my school, and from preschool through high school graduation, I had such low self-esteem and always thought of myself as an "outsider" looking in. As I was being tossed from one home to another, a "rap sheet" listed the living conditions of the previous foster home in which I lived. Rather than being a safety net, it became a permission slip for the foster father of my new setting to have his way with me. Victim of sexual abuse? Check. Child molestation? Check. Physical abuse? Check.

The "list" spelled it all out, and little did I know that I was running from one abusive home to another. I was constantly belittled, called a "slut," "whore," "loose," etc. It was the same drill meeting the next "parents." "Will I be raped or beaten here, too? Is this what normal families do?" Social services made many personal promises, but there was never any action that resulted in anything different other than a new street address. We were the "smelly, poor kids," and so we grew to think this was the way it was going to be forever.

One of our first placements was in a big brown house with a long walkway. The social worker said the family was nice and that my sister and I would love it there. There were lots of toys, and we didn't have to move far from our friends or go to a different school, so we were excited initially. We could have occasional visitations with our mother and were told that we would eventually be placed back with her when she got better.

Little did we know at the time that meeting our new "family" was the beginning of hell. The mother had bulging eyes with a face full of anger. We were scared to death! It didn't take long to determine the only role we played was to be her maids. We became the burdens she didn't want. She gave us very little food. In fact, when we cleared the table, we would take food off the plates and lick them clean. It was so intimidating having someone watch us eat. She would say, "Close your mouth when you eat!" I was sure mine was closed, but she hit me so hard with the back of her hand that I tasted blood. She then pulled me off the chair and threw me down, saying, "If you're going to eat like a dog, then you can eat off the floor." She then tipped the plate upside down and dumped my food on the floor. This was only the start of our nightmares.

My sister and I lived in constant fear. One day when we were cleaning the house after a party, I lost my footing on some spilled beer on the floor, and I went for a tumble. In the process, I knocked over an ashtray and watched the ashes and cigarettes hit the floor.

"Didn't I tell you to clean this mess up? Stand up, you stupid little bitch! When I tell you something, you need to do it!"

I wanted to cry, but I knew the rules about crying and having tears in my eyes. She reached on the table for a pack of cigarettes and a box of matches and continued, "Put your hands out in front of you. Now turn them over. I told you to clean this place, and what do you do? You make more of a mess of it."

Robotically I did what she told me to do and turned my palms up. She lit the cigarette and blew the smoke in my face. The pain from her slap on my hand ran through to my fingertips as she proceeded to turn the cigarette upside down and burn it into my left hand. When I jumped from the heat, she grabbed my hair and said, "I said stand still! You want to drop cigarettes? You won't ever do it again, will you?"

She was very particular about how we needed to do the dishes. The glasses were to be washed with plenty of soap and water and dried with a white floral hand towel. If the glasses had any marks or lint on them, they had to be rewashed. I now had an open burn on the back of my hand as I focused on making sure the table was spotless and everything went where it was supposed to go. She was in a rage throwing things, and my sister and I got really scared. As we were drying the glasses, my sister looked at me, and as if in slow motion, a glass hit the floor. Now it was her turn to be punished.

At this time, I was seven years old, and my sister was barely six. Though I tried to protect her, the monster grabbed a cast iron pan off the stove and hit my sister in the back of her head. As she fell forward from her chair, she struck another blow to my sister's head, which made her hit the floor with a hard thud. Sissy didn't cry or even make a sound, and her body went completely limp. The monster pushed me out of the way and proceeded to take her lifeless body up to the bathtub and fill it with ice-cold water.

"Sissy!! Sissy!! Please wake up!" I was fearful that she was about to drown, so I held her little head above the water and tried to keep her eyes open. With a tub full of blood and cold water, I could hear the monster on the phone pleading for someone to come for help. I leaned closer to see if my sister was still breathing and made a promise out loud to her: "Sissy, if you wake up, I promise that we will run away for real this time and make our own home in the woods. No one will ever find us again, but you have to wake up, OK?"

The story I heard being told on the phone was that my sister had fallen off a chair and hit her head hard against the floor. If the monster showed fear, I knew it had to be bad. The monster threw a towel on the floor to clean up the blood, but I wouldn't move from my sister's side, so she dragged me across the floor. For the first time, I kicked her, and she released me as I ran to reach for my sister's head, now underwater.

As the tub was unplugged, she said, "See what you little bastards made me do! If only you would listen and do what you're told! You dumb little bitches make my life a living hell! Kiss your sister goodbye because you're never going to see her again! Because she's dead! She's a dead little bitch like you're going to be next."

I was then taken to a dark crawl space where the monster taped my legs, hands, and face. The tape was so tight around my nose that I could barely breathe. Soon I heard people taking my sister somewhere to be treated. I heard, "Are you going to follow us there?" The monster replied, "I'll come as soon as I call my husband."

We had been instructed that if we had any marks on our body, we were to say it was an accident. I don't know how long I was confined in the dark crawl space, but when I awakened, I had to pee but couldn't move due to being bound up. I managed to produce enough spit to loosen the tape around my face, but I couldn't hold back any longer, so I urinated in my pajamas. I knew there would be vengeance when the monster returned. So many thoughts were racing through my head, the most prominent being the persistent question of whether my sister was still alive. I dreamed that a magic fairy would come, and I would plead for her to let me out of the box in which I was trapped.

The next day when the monster returned home, she violently pulled off the tape bound around my legs and hands that had turned blue from the tight wrapping. My pajamas were covered in dried blood, and when she pulled the tape from my face and head, both skin and hair came off with a painful tug. She was disgusted by the urine smell and proceeded to degrade me with the foul language and humiliation I had come to expect. Then came such horrific kicking that I didn't think I'd ever walk again. In her rage, she whipped me with a leather strap that made me feel like I was going to die. I was brought to the shower, where my P.J.s were ripped off my body, and I was instructed to turn around slowly. I figured she wanted to see the bruises on my body so she could concoct another story to clear herself from being charged with abuse.

My sight was blurry from blood in one eye and soap in the other. Then she began pouring a liquid over my head and into my cut eye. I screamed as the liquid Pine-Sol dripped down my body. "Wash up, you dirty little thing. I hate you! I can't stand you!" she hissed.

She then pulled me into my bedroom and continued to dress my eye wound to stop the bleeding. Suddenly her mood changed, and she began acting sweetly as she told me I needed to be better so this wouldn't happen again. She brought me a glass of water and a peanut butter sandwich as I sat at the end of the bed. As she combed my hair, she said I would get a new haircut before I went back to school. I then asked about my sister, and she told me I had better not tell anybody about what happened or else! She then left me behind a closed bedroom door, and I cried myself to sleep. I remember wishing that I would fall asleep and never wake up again.

The next day I woke up in such pain, I didn't want to live. I could barely walk, and I was black and blue from the top of my thigh to the back of my knee. My bruises were hard as a rock, and my skin and scalp were very sensitive to the touch. After shampooing, the monster was almost comforting me as she began to cut my hair. As I saw her drop a large chunk of my hair in the sink, I was sad because my mom used to tell me it was so pretty and that it smelled like sunshine. She cut my bangs just enough to avoid exposing the cut above my eye. I was then informed that I wouldn't be returning to school until I could walk better.

• • • •

The day finally came when Yvonne was allowed to return to school because her bruises had healed enough to be largely undetectable, and she was walking without concern. The monster began laying out beautiful clothes, like high neck ruffled tops and long pants, and preparing Yvonne for what to say when people asked why she had been away from school for such a long time: she had had the flu, there were bugs in her hair, she had tripped and cut her eye, etc. Her sister was still in the hospital, and of course, she was told to say that her sister had had a bad fall that caused a head injury. The lies and secrets continued to mount, but at least Yvonne had the opportunity to be free a few hours a day at school rather than in the prison she experienced with her foster mother.

You might say that a bee sting saved Yvonne's life the day she returned to school. Recess had ended, and there was an apparent frenzy on the playground when a swarm of bees invaded the space, and Yvonne was stung. She was brought to the school nurse, who quickly observed her allergic reaction to bees as she carefully removed the stinger. Through this incident, the school nurse contacted the social worker to question Yvonne about the bruises she noticed while removing the bee sting. The social worker assured Yvonne that she could trust the nurse to be responsible with any information Yvonne shared with her and that she'd work to protect Yvonne from any further abuse as best she could.

Yvonne was soon removed from her foster home but wondered where she'd be placed next and questioned whether she could truly dream of a safe, secure home that could love and nurture her. The answer was "Yes!" and her next caretaker would be a sweet, loving older woman who loved her like a granddaughter. Yvonne describes this woman as being almost magical, and from the ages of seven to 13, Yvonne flourished in her care. Biking, playing, camping, swimming, and being loved by her new foster mother's extended family was a standard agenda in Yvonne's new life. She felt beautiful and loved. The woman's deep faith in God also inspired Yvonne's personal walk in believing Jesus loved her, too. But little did Yvonne know, a new storm was brewing, and it began with babysitting her cousins.

After the children were asleep, a new male monster emerged as the children's father escorted Yvonne to his bedroom. She kept her eyes closed as his tongue slid down her body, and she could smell his breath on her face. The man was her foster mother's son, who tickled her stomach, gave her a whisker rub, and then fondled her chest and in between her legs. Yvonne ran from him and locked the door in her foster mother's room, but then he broke open the door and pinned her to the bed. He laughed and breathed heavily as she was crushed by his weight, unable to breathe or escape.

• • • •

YVONNE SPEAKS AGAIN

"Why hadn't I gone to town with Grandma and my sister?" I questioned myself. Immediately my eyes found a picture in her room that said, "Trust in the Lord." Our home was filled with pictures of Jesus. I saw His face smiling at me, and in my mind, I said, "Please help me, Jesus!"

Immediately I was filled with strength and boldness while I kicked, screamed, hit, and scratched him. I dug my nails into his back, and he yelled, "Stop, Let go! I'll let you up. I won't tell anyone what you did?" (What I DID?) "I promise! Please stop biting, and I'll leave you alone!" he screamed. I looked back at the picture of Jesus, and I unlocked my jaws.

He continued to fix his clothes and pleaded, "I'm so sorry. Don't tell Grandma what happened, and I promise never to bother you again. OK?"

I stood there staring into the mirror, looking at an ugly four-eyed girl with curly hair looking back at me. I looked out the window as his truck drove down the road. I knew he was gone and wouldn't be back anytime soon.

• • • •

Over a period of days, Yvonne's foster mother was devastated to find out through Yvonne's confession that her son had been sexually abusing Yvonne. She was mortified, which led her to contact social services and have social services remove Yvonne from the home of safety and security she and her sister had known and loved for five years. With her 14th birthday right around the corner, Yvonne faced a new high school, a new home, new friends, and, yes, another new family.

To make a long story short, Yvonne went through a period of drinking and rebellion, which took her into a recovery program for 60 days and, yes, another foster home. In an intoxicated state, Yvonne spilled her life history to a police officer who became her next foster father and safety advocate. Eventually, the police officer became ill and was taken to a nursing home where her biological father lived. There she was able to heal by addressing her father and forgiving him for what he had done to her.

Despite all the trauma she endured, Yvonne managed to graduate high school with honors and was offered a college scholarship to an Ivy League school. Unfortunately, she ended up in an abusive relationship with a man she met and fell in love with at the age of 18 and with whom she had two children. The grooming process that led to abuse began with sweet talk and promises that never transpired. He dictated how he wanted her to touch him and what sounds he wanted her to make during their sexual acts, and he also recorded many of their encounters. Yvonne was told how beautiful she was, something she had never heard from a male, which initially caused her to stay. When the abuse got too much to handle, she contacted a women's shelter where she could escape with her children and start a new life.

YVONNE TODAY

Today, Yvonne devotes herself to helping others who have endured a similar path of abuse and exploitation and is an author and speaker whose whole story is told in her 2019 memoir *In the Hands of An Abuser* (Griffin, 2019). Yvonne credits intense therapy and a return to her spiritual roots as huge contributors to her attaining freedom from her past. She carries an incredible level of resilience and passion for equipping the broken and pointing them toward wholeness. She rewrote toxic mental narratives and now thinks and speaks a message of hope and love. She is soon to release her second book. Indeed, she is finally living abundantly in service to others as she pursues a career in women's ministry.

 POINTS TO PONDER

1. Numerous acts that took place in Yvonne's life were unconscionable. Consider the following four vital variables that contribute to our behavior: (a) People in our sphere of influence; (b) Culture; (c) Biology (genetics); and (d) Cognitive thought processes or mindset. How did these variables play out in Yvonne's early life?

2. How and where did "the system" fail Yvonne in multiple ways? How can we be proactive now to ensure that other children in foster care can avoid the heinous brutality Yvonne experienced repeatedly?

3. How does Yvonne's story encourage you to advocate for children surviving abuse?

CHAPTER SEVEN
EXPLOITED VULNERABILITIES
CHRISTA SPEAKS

> *"Though she be but little, she is fierce."*
> - WILLIAM SHAKESPEARE

Individuals who have suffered abuse, endured complex trauma, or have mental health conditions can be more vulnerable to fall victim to various forms of exploitation. Human trafficking is one such form of exploitation that has become a worldwide epidemic. By definition, human trafficking is the control and exploitation of people for profit. It includes any child under 18 involved in the sex industry, any adult age 18 or older who is coerced, deceived, or forced into engaging in commercial sex acts, and lastly, anyone subjected to forced labor. In the United States, California ranks as the top state for reported human trafficking cases, with Texas and Florida ranking second and third, respectively (Senesac, 2021). According to one sou rce, 25% of the 40 million victims worldwide who are trafficked annually are children, and in the U.S., over 50% of human trafficking cases involve children (Child Liberation Foundation, 2020). Additionally, globally, human trafficking is a $150 billion a year enterprise according to UNICEF USA and is the second-largest global enterprise (UNICEF USA, 2017).

The dynamics of a crime like human trafficking are extremely diverse and complex. Predators look to exploit victims' vulnerabilities which can range significantly based on a perpetrator's intent and a victim's age, gender, region, or country in which they reside. In this body of work, we focus our attention on the epidemic of child sex trafficking, also known as commercial sexual exploitation, in the United States. As we will discuss in Part 2, adverse childhood experiences (ACEs) are directly linked to human trafficking, creating significant vulnerabilities that predators look for in potential victims.

The complex trauma many children and adolescents endured in the foster care system provides traffickers with ample opportunities to recruit, exploit, and violate this demographic. A report from the Human Rights Project for Girls, Georgetown Law Center on Poverty and Inequality, and Foundation for Women titled "The Sexual Abuse to Prison Pipeline" found that girls who grow up in the instability of the child welfare system, particularly those placed in multiple homes, are "vulnerable to the manipulation of traffickers who promise to love and care for them. Indeed, some traffickers purposely troll for youth in certain group homes because they are aware of this vulnerability" (Saar et al., n.d.).

When adolescents run away or flee an abusive home or environment, one-third of them are recruited into sexual exploitation within the first 48 hours of fleeing (Juneau & Banta, 2018). The National Center for Campus Public Safety also reported that the average age of exposure and entry into commercial sexual exploitation is 12 years old (Juneau & Banta, 2018). When someone has been repeatedly abused in childhood, they can unknowingly find themselves in exploitative situations because they have become desensitized to the abuse or have no support system. The Polaris Project, a data-driven social justice movement fighting sex and labor trafficking, states that "every year, children and young adults are compelled into sex trafficking in the United States. While trafficking affects all demographics, traffickers frequently target individuals who lack strong support networks, are facing financial strains, have experienced violence in the past, or are marginalized by society. Without adequate community support, youth who identify as lesbian, gay, bisexual, transgender, queer, or questioning (LGBTQ) may be at particular risk for sex trafficking. When faced with fewer resources, employment opportunities, or social support, LGBTQ youth away from home must find ways to meet their basic needs. Traffickers may seek to exploit these vulnerabilities to compel youth into commercial sex" (Polaris, n.d.).

Both sex and labor trafficking use the same techniques to trap individuals into servitude. A trafficker will often use force, fraud, and coercion to trap someone into involuntary servitude or debt bondage through using them in commercial sex acts or labor-intensive jobs. Sex traffickers use these three tactics to manipulate their victims into engaging in commercial sex acts. First, they exploit the traumatic experiences their victims have endured. Force is used to break any resistance a victim might have toward sex acts, and can include heinous actions such as beatings, torture, rape and other acts of sexual violence, forced abortions, violently using restraints to subdue victims, denying food, water, and medical care, removing or harming children if the victim is a parent, and deliberately concealing the victims' whereabouts to family and friends (Litam, 2017; U.S. Department of State, 2007). The DEA states that "human traffickers often use drugs as bait to recruit people who have a substance use disorder. Or, conversely, traffickers use drugs as a means of control over their victims – to force compliance, harder work, longer hours, or to keep them drugged out so they do not attempt escape" (Forget, 2021).

As many victims of sex trafficking are often fleeing abusive situations and need shelter, food, and a job, traffickers exploit these vulnerabilities and use them to lure their targets into commercial sex work. It is common for a trafficker to promise a victim steady employment, stability, and money. Sadly, many victims never see these promises and often have their wages withheld while they are treated in inhumane and horrific ways.

Coercion is another tactic that traffickers use to scare their victims into submission. They will threaten their victims with physical or sexual abuse and often threaten to harm the victims' family and friends if they fail to comply with the traffickers' demands (Litam, 2017). A study done by

Polaris Project reports, "Traffickers manipulate their victims beginning with an initial period of false love and feigned affection. This initial period is critical to attaining long-term mind-control and often includes warmth, gifts, compliments, sexual/physical intimacy, and elaborate promises of a better life, fast money, and future luxuries. Traffickers purposefully and premeditatedly target vulnerabilities (e.g., runaways, wards of the state), and purposefully target minors due to naivete, virginity, and youthful appearance" (Polaris Project, n.d.).

There were several red flags and warning signs along the way that put Christa at risk for exploitation. Unfortunately, many of Christa's teachers did not see the trauma she carried and focused instead on her aggressive behavior. Had one adult inquired about her home life, they may have identified the imminent danger Christa was in daily.

• • • •

Wild, different, problematic, and wired for explosiveness is how Christa describes her younger self. As she speaks candidly about her school experiences from age four to 17, it is clear she fell through the cracks of the educational system. Instead of receiving needed support, she was isolated and shamed for being a "troubled child." Many teachers, administrative staff, and students excluded her. This was also an indicator of the limited awareness and needed services for high-risk students like Christa in the 80s. The conventional services offered were either total isolation from other students in the classroom or a space in the back of the room where students labeled "troubled" would do their own thing. In a traditional setting, teachers were not equipped to handle the intensity of a child-like Christa who was aggressive, edgy, hyperactive, and high-needs. This resulted in inadequate learning conditions and little instructional time with qualified adults.

Of course, it was not Christa's deliberate plan to come to school and disrupt everyone's space. She didn't choose to be purposefully obstinate, staging fits and creating chaos in the classroom just for kicks. The predominant, underlying cause of her constant acting out was a vulnerability in an unstable home with an alcoholic mother who was out of control and unreliable in every way. Her learned behavior from an early age followed her into the classroom, out on the playground, and into every community interaction. She was at risk and raised in a second-generation sexually abusive home. It appears that the educators in her life weren't equipped with the skills and resources needed to fully support her in the ways she needed to be supported.

Christa's mother modeled what she experienced growing up as a victim of childhood abuse herself. Yet Christa quickly responds that her mother was also very loving, even though she was unreliable and inconsistent as a parent. By the age of 15, Christa's mom carried many hidden secrets, one of which was an unwanted pregnancy with no one to tell or support her. By the age of 17, she returned to the hard life of the streets as a teen prostitute, though that term is not used as much anymore for underaged victims of sexual abuse. By 18, her biological father swooped in to rescue Christa's mother, who was by this time addicted to heroin. Shortly after his "rescue," the two were married, and they moved in with his mother.

Christa's paternal grandmother was a controlling force who made it clear that there should be no additional children in her son's future. Despite this advice, Christa's mother got pregnant again the following year. Upon learning she was pregnant, Christa's mother was overwhelmed with shame and starved herself to keep the new baby's growth under the radar as long as possible. During this time, Christa's mother wanted to believe her husband would stand by her, but because of her past trauma, she could not discern between safety and danger, which led to her running away. Her circumstances left her feeling stuck and unsafe, with no other options but to run. This insecurity carried over into future relationships with men as well.

Christa recalls an early life of instability, poverty, and constantly running from hotels to apartments where child services were less likely to get involved.

By the age of five, her sister Isabella took an empty bowl from room to room at one apartment complex, asking for food to feed her toddler sister, who was starving not only from malnutrition but also emotional care and attention. Isabella, a needy preschool child herself, became the advocate to feed, clothe, and change diapers while their mother fed her drug and alcohol addictions.

Around the age of three to five, Christa's mother worked at a run-down topless bar where she and her sister were allowed to sit at the bar while their mom worked. The kids survived off bar food, primarily pistachios during the day, and after her mother's shift ended, they were allowed a little free time to try on the inappropriate clothes fit for the strippers dancing on the wooden floor. Both girls developed tough exteriors at an early age to survive. However, Christa's sister's survival tactic was to behave perfectly and take on a caregiver role to ensure the family did not fall apart, while Christa's survival tactic became more open defiance.

• • • •

CHRISTA SPEAKS

As a petite, cute, little "gremlin," I recall being labeled a "motor mouth" in school, something that won approval amongst the tough adult circles I knew as "family" outside of school. This served me well as I met many different men rotating through whichever temporary front door happened to be home for the time being. I was bound and determined to survive, so the message I told myself was that I could talk my way through anything. I was a spitfire because I had to be. What I often heard my family and teachers say was, "She sure is cute, but she's not very smart." That's the tape I replayed in my head, so when I sat at my school desk, my brain went offline, my eyes glazed over, and I sat inattentive and despondent regarding anything academic. I spent my life figuring out how to make certain no one would mess with me.

It was normal for my sister and me to be two among a growing sea of 10-

20 kids when other dancers and strippers left their children at our house. My mom would watch these kids anytime, day or night, and ignored signs that other sitters would have reported. Most of them were tough boys, and in their presence, I acted indestructible. Historically, these were children who all had high ACE scores as victims themselves, and this was my posse. At the time, I exhibited hyperactive behaviors at school, so my mother was called to take me to the doctor, where I was diagnosed with hypoglycemia. Mother tried her best to wean me off sugar, but I learned to space out and do my own thing while in the classroom. I was "that kid" – a wild, problematic, and vulnerable child who had a unique mind that thought differently than any of my classmates.

A saving grace for my overly active sister and me was going to gymnastics, where we could blow off our energy in a productive way. Our coach was wonderful and saw our potential to go straight to the top in competition due to our natural abilities. Gradually we were invited to train 20 hours a week with the team, and we became very successful. Since I was a couple of years younger than most, I never felt part of the social "crowd" in the gym. I was there to work hard and was fueled by the positive comments and rewards I received from those who coached me. That motivated me to excel, but it also took me to the brink of obsessiveness. It became my life-long dream to become a successful Olympian. It was a military-like environment that offered structure and stability, and I loved the mental toughness required to perform with excellence.

By the age of 11, I had become very performance-driven, but I was failing miserably at school. I still lived in poverty and had no friends. Then my mother divorced, and things quickly went downhill, coming to a crashing end. For both my sister and me to receive ongoing gymnastics lessons, the coach negotiated a contract with my mother to clean the gym after everyone left. She usually appeared wasted and in a stupor. She never watched us rehearse, nor did she attend our competitions or exhibitions, so the day my mother appeared unexpectedly in the middle of our practice, I knew right away what heart-breaking news was to be announced. I was performing on the bars when she entered. Immediately I jumped off the equipment and announced, "I quit." I knew my mother's message would indicate the end of the only thing I lived for. It was at this point I wanted to give up on life. The one personal success I had control of as a skilled gymnast was being stripped away from me, and I was devastated.

It was at this time I became an oppositional defiant preteen. My mantra was "Bring it on!" and self-destruction became my middle name. The world meant absolutely nothing to me, and I had learned to normalize pain and suffering. My brain began to confuse harm and trauma for love, and my self-worth was so low that self-punishment seemed appropriate because I didn't believe I deserved to be happy.

My mother wasn't functional at all during this time. I learned that humor and aggressiveness could be my ticket in life, so my highest value was to be an entertainer. Mom would be gone all night, so when midnight struck, I would break out, too. Even though I got into all kinds of juvenile trouble, like breaking into vehicles, I was still a very naïve 12-year-old in many ways. I was running around with kids who were much older than I was, but they favored their tough, feisty companion because I could handle myself well. In fact, at one point, they lined me up against a wall and threw rocks at me as I tried to dodge them. I heard one of the boys say, "You are going to kill her!" The response was always, "Nah; she's indestructible!" as they continued to punch my gut to see how much I could tolerate.

By the age of 13, I had developed into a troubled, chaotic tomboy who thrived being with "da boys." I had one very good male friend at school, and I was failing all subjects miserably. I had not made any connections with my teachers, so I checked out. I was not about to let any adult mess with my mind or heart, so I simply shut everyone in authority out of my life. At this time, my friend and I spent all our free time together away from school. I do believe I was still "reachable" by all standards, but I didn't feel safe or trusting enough for others to stand in the gap for me. I lived like an adult who did whatever I wanted, although I was privately craving for someone to stop the madness.

At this time, I was still a virgin and very naïve. One night, my friend crossed the line by raping me at a house party where his drinking influenced his actions. This rocked my world since he had stood by me as my number one platonic friend. There was never even the slightest suggestion of being sexually involved with him until that event. That incident left me confused and further violated, as I distanced myself from him and then suffered the lies that spread like wildfire across the school grounds, including "The little whore gave me crabs!"

I didn't even know what crabs were! This had been my very first sexual encounter with anyone. I could hear my mother's voice calling me a slut, tramp, and whore in the back of her mind. Now I knew what my mother had been describing to me all along. But the fighter in me was not about to crumble, so I became numb and even tougher to protect myself.

• • • •

With a report card full of Fs and comments that indicated retention, Christa remained disengaged in school. In 7th grade, she was sent repeatedly to the "time out" room with the other "disruptive" kids. In 8th grade, teachers often sat her in the back of the room, where she pulled out coloring books and was allowed to create her own fun all day long, without any academic expectations.

As 9th grade approached, a new program was introduced to accommodate 15 of the most high-needs students from neighboring middle schools. This consisted of three females and 12 males. Rather than keeping the girls together, the administration decided to haul in three portable buildings that functioned in total isolation from the other students on campus. Each free-standing building would house one obstinate female, with nine defiant, angry males, taught by unskilled, retired teachers on sub pay. Christa completely checked out in this environment and went on strike on her own behalf. Eventually, Christa got the news that she would be passed on to high school due to the overcrowded school despite her failing academic performance and her perpetual defiant behaviors.

By this time, Christa was determined to show everyone who was boss. A steady diet of obstinate behavior included cussing out teachers, throwing books at them, and flipping over desks in the classroom. Interruption, defiance, and power became Christa's game plan. And somehow, her behavior continued with few formal consequences.

At this time, Christa's mother was going through bankruptcy but decided to go on one last shopping spree, bringing home all kinds of expensive, over-sexualized clothing for her daughter to wear. It was not unusual for Christa to take off on a bus, be gone for days on end, sleeping in bushes, under trucks, in garages, or wherever she could find a place to lay her head.

• • • •

CHRISTA SPEAKS AGAIN

By the time I reached 15, I was a hot mess, full of trauma-induced circumstances. And I didn't care about anything! My mother was threatening to leave us, and eventually, she tried to take her own life, so my adopted father attempted to take my sister and me, along with his four teen boys, and move us to the beach. This sounded like a good plan to me, but all it did was heighten my criminal activity, which was already at an all-time high. All four "step-brothers" had also been traumatized and were now selling illegal drugs. Additionally, we all got involved in stealing cars, breaking into properties, robbing stores, and many other criminal activities, which eventually led me to juvenile court. Now, my life was an ongoing fight, and education was the lowest priority.

I was so desperate that I pleaded with my mother to let me come home to her, and she finally gave in. Back at home, I continued to fail miserably in school, with very few credits and no intervention on the school front. I lasted six months in my mother's home when I couldn't handle her physical abuse any longer. In addition, I had a five-year-old brother who I was expected to babysit 24/7, and I was not about to commit to that type of infringement on my loose and free lifestyle. In theory, she tried to be a good mother by working and attending regular A.A. meetings. Still, any person in their right mind would not leave an explosive, undependable teen to babysit a child seven days a week.

In the past, I had experienced a couple of foster home situations that I hated, so I was bound and determined to take matters into my own hands and find myself a family I could call my own. I was a brave little bugger, and it didn't bother me one bit to ask a total stranger if they had a place in their home for me. I wasn't close to anyone at this time, but I remembered a girl from school who I felt comfortable asking if she and her mother would take me in. To have some leverage so the courts would not file a neglect charge, my mother tore the tags off some expensive clothes I had stolen, brought them to the police, and pleaded with them to arrest me. Even though she had made attempts at sobriety, they hadn't stuck. So she showed up at the police station that day, utterly wasted and suffering from borderline personality disorder. Shortly after this, I was put into juvenile court, where I was stripped naked and sprayed down for lice, given the proverbial orange jail suit that made me feel so degraded and worthless, and then strapped into shackles.

While in DJJ (Department of Juvenile Justice), I was allowed to make one call that would be directed to my "boyfriend," a 19-year-old five years my senior who worked in construction and had a horrible reputation for being vile and corrupt. He would beat me, drag me by my hair on the coarse pavement, pull me out of the passenger window of his car, and bruise my body from top to bottom. While in court, my foster parent showed up and told me she and her daughter would take me to California to start a new life. In the midnight hour, my so-called boyfriend convinced me to abandon that plan and come live with him instead. So I did. It was the worst mistake of my life. I was totally controlled and in bondage in his home, and nobody knew where I was. Absolutely no one! I had used up all my lifelines, and I was trapped. He had planned it that way, which started my life of sex trafficking.

I was only 15 ½ at the time, and I carried on this secretive relationship with him under his parents' roof. I was given a large man's shirt and a pair of baggy jogging pants and locked in a room with red and black walls and closed blinds. I was unable to go anywhere because he knew I might run. Within 24 hours of moving in with him, he began to constantly belittle me and tell me how much he hated me.

Within a week, I started devising a plan to escape. I thought, "You can have my body, but you can't have my mind!" On one outing with him, I tried jumping out of a moving car but failed, as he dragged me down the street and back into the car with a vengeance. I often tried to fight back, but I convinced myself that I'd never escape alive after many failed attempts. And that's when my body and brain completely shut down. I stopped eating, talking, and functioning. I was entirely at his mercy and in total submission and desperation.

At this time, I met a woman called the "wife" among a group of construction workers who were work companions with him. He had arranged to have me entertain a large group of men from work. He forced me to do horrible things; it makes me panic thinking about it, and much of it I have blocked out of my memory. All I remember was there was so much white substance flying in the air, and it made me sick! Of the two and a half months of the summer of 10th grade, I only remember two specific nights; the rest is entirely blocked from my memory.

I decided that the only way to survive the brutality, sexual exploitation, and trafficking would be to make a mental shift and go along with his deviant plans. Once I proved I could be trusted, the "wife" took me to work with her, where I was constantly watched and monitored in my little telemarketing space. I was labor trafficked as well, even though I didn't know what that meant at the time. In the month I worked in the office, I never received a check, but I did begin asking the "wife" if she would help me escape. The answer was always no because her job was to keep me in line, and her life would be jeopardized if she didn't comply. The environment was so controlled and prison-like that I never dared use the phone in my cubicle to call out for help. If I had done this, it would have ended poorly, I told myself.

Out of desperation, I had memorized a telephone number of an acquaintance just in case I could break free from the total confinement I was trapped in. After finally giving in, the "wife" and I devised a story that I had asked to use a toilet and then fled on foot without her knowing. In actuality, I was dropped off at a telephone booth by her and called my school acquaintance, who came to rescue me from the bondage. The school year had already been in session for a month, and it was two weeks after my 16th birthday. After staying with my friend for seven days, I reconnected with my mother, who encouraged me to come home and obtain a restraining order against the man. This was when I developed an angry, unhealthy attachment disorder, and my rage became uncontrollable. I had failed miserably in the traditional education system, so I quit school. Later I got my GED, which gave me a sense of academic accomplishment. But some of the most challenging days of life were ahead.

• • • •

CHRISTA TODAY

Soon after the age of 18, Christa's life hit rock bottom. At this low point, she decided to participate in a year-long addiction recovery program that changed the course of her life. Christa recalls that when she took her eyes off her own trauma-centered life, she began to truly see and feel the hurts of others. Out of this newfound compassion, she was compelled to take action.

Returning to school with a renewed mindset, learning became a passion as she chose to better her life by entering college and pursuing higher education. After receiving a master's degree in mental health counseling, she was led to establish a holistic, Christ-centered counseling and wellness center for trafficked and exploited women named Into the Jordan. The organization's purpose is to empower survivors through healing, education, employment, and stable housing.

After founding Into the Jordan, she became the executive director of anti-trafficking at One More Child, an organization bringing healing and hope to child victims of domestic sex trafficking through wrap-around care and services. After a fruitful season, she resigned to launch SaltWater Therapist, a new trauma therapy program for survivors centered around her love for the outdoors. Christa is a dedicated and compassionate woman who shares her experience as a trafficking survivor, her clinical expertise, and years of growth to continuously improve the services available to those being sold and exploited by others.

A video version of Christa Lynn's life story can be found online (https://vimeo.com/291571128). Christa's dynamic energy, authentic, survivor-leader voice, and professional expertise truly make a difference across the globe.

POINTS TO PONDER

1. People in our sphere of influence, like family, can contribute to our behavior. Reflect on how Christa's family relationships influenced her early life.

2. How can childhood trauma create significant vulnerabilities in potential victims that sexual predators seek to exploit?

3. How did Christa show resilience and survive abuse, neglect, and sexual exploitation?

4. How have the stories of Christa and the other survivors changed your perspective of the future life of a victimized child and the impact they can make on society for good?

PART 2
THE STRATEGIES

CHAPTER EIGHT
WRITING ON THE WALL

In the middle of the night, a woman flees from her abusive husband and the father of her four-year-old son, Ted, not realizing that her act of self-preservation would put her son in direct contact with the man who had inflicted so much physical and emotional pain upon her. As Ted's mother escapes the heavy hand of her husband, Ted is left in the wreckage with no one to advocate for him. His welfare is disregarded as his father begins drumming negative messages into his brain. Ted was told not to get too close to anyone because they might leave and that he was a terrible person. The secrets and abandonment issues began to scar Ted's life deeply from an early age, and as he entered preschool, Ted found himself alone most of the time with no playmates his age to keep him company. Ted's father began sexually abusing him at four years old as the two slept in the same bed together.

Ted's father had become a dominating presence in Ted's life and demanded submission to every one of his rules. Whenever Ted opposed these rules, he was greeted with a slap in the face, cruel put-downs, abusive language, or a beating with the belt. As Ted grew older, he saw his father's excessive drinking and physical abuse as the primary reasons for his mother's departure, despite being told by his father that Ted was the reason his mother left.

Ted had unknowingly been groomed at a young age by his father. By not being allowed to play with other kids his age, his father deliberately placed him into contact with sexual predators. Ted's father routinely reasoned that Ted needed to be around older men to learn how to survive and think for himself. As Ted was surrounded by these older men in his apartment complex, he was forced to perform sexual acts for them. Ted's silence was bought with gifts such as bicycles, candy, and money, and he never confided in his teachers about the abuse he was enduring. By the age of 16, however, Ted had had enough. He and his father had an explosive argument that prompted his father to drive Ted 20 miles outside of the city limits and throw him onto a busy interstate highway in the dead of winter. Ted had nowhere to go with only a few dollars and a backpack to his name.

Ted would turn to the skills he had acquired at home to survive, knowing that he could problem-solve his way out of almost any situation. Earning a few bucks to get him to the next town, he hitchhiked to a community that did not know him for five hours. The entirety of Ted's life was centered around finding odd jobs that offered payment through meals and accommodations. He often hitchhiked to another community looking for work once a job ended. However, he ended up being repeatedly coerced into engaging in sexual acts with men in exchange for shelter. Ted didn't view this as out of the ordinary, as his upbringing had normalized sex trafficking.

When I first met Ted, he was 16 years old, and I had no idea he had survived such despicable acts of abuse and sexual exploitation. He frequented the community youth center where I was a director and would initiate mature conversations for his age. Impressed by his maturity and politeness, I offered him a job in the concession area. For what may have been the first time in his life, Ted interacted with kids around his age and formed friendships.

Ted eventually began confiding in me a bit more. I learned about his traumatic upbringing through our talks and that his current living situation was also toxic and dangerous. He had connected with a manager of a local pizza establishment who was feeding and housing him in exchange for sex. I immediately advocated for his placement in a stable foster home. Things had seemed to be turning around for Ted. He appeared to be adjusting well in his foster home and was excelling at work.

I began giving Ted more responsibilities at work. Shortly after, I started noticing that the cash drawer at the concession stand was not balancing and found missing pieces of expensive technology shortly afterward. Ted's admission of theft carried a stiff penalty of immediate termination from his job and placement into juvenile court. Despite these initial infractions, Ted would continue to commit felonies such as hacking into the school's district computer network and pawning numerous technological items. However, his gravest offense came when he engaged in sexual acts with teenagers from the community who reported him to the police.

Had Ted had an advocate who noticed these early signs of abuse, he might not have had to endure such unconscionable acts of sexual exploitation and violence. In the early years, had there been an observant teacher, nurse, doctor, or school administrator, the abuse may have stopped, and Ted might not have gone on to initiate inappropriate sexual relations with others.

Though he continued the harmful behaviors that got him into trouble after leaving our community, Ted is now working toward living a productive life and has broken the cycle of abuse. Today, he is working through his trauma with the support of his partner, has reconnected with his mother, and continues to move forward on his journey of healing. Ted's dedication to rewriting the abusive narratives that continually played in his thoughts shows us that trauma survivors can create new positive mindsets that improve their quality of life.

When a first responder such as a nurse, teacher, doctor, or school administrator intervenes and reports suspected abuse of children, they are often identifying adverse childhood experiences (ACEs). Had a trustworthy adult intervened and gotten Ted to open up about the abuse he was enduring at home as a young child, they would have possibly taken note of several ACEs that could have been addressed early on and prevented further victimization.

• • • •

ADVERSE CHILDHOOD EXPERIENCES

Adverse Childhood Experiences (ACEs) are traumatic events that youth under 18 experience, including abuse and neglect. ACEs are essential identifiers of the long-term health risks of childhood trauma survivors and can facilitate early intervention methods that prevent future violence, victimization, and perpetration. ACEs cannot predict a child's outcome, and the presence of ACEs in a child's life does not automatically mean they will encounter all of the health and safety risks associated with their trauma (Harris, 2014). Dr. Nadine Burke Harris' work around ACEs has shaped much of the information available on the topic today.

The ACE assessment, which is readily available online and in the resources section of the book's website, has become a global screening tool to identify abuse survivors and implement treatment options for those survivors. The score on the ACE assessment directly correlates to the severity of the childhood adversities by tallying different forms of abuse, neglect, and other traumatic events experienced in childhood. A high ACE score carries risks of developing chronic health conditions, housing and employment insecurities, mental and emotional health challenges, and early death. While the ACE checklist does not have the power to predict an individual's outcome based on the traumas they faced in childhood, it can provide a blueprint for identifying potential risk factors in adulthood resulting from those traumas such as depression, anxiety, severe headaches, and heart disease (Bethell et al., 2019).

ACEs are categorized into three types: abuse, neglect, and household dysfunction. Abuse includes physical, emotional, and sexual violations, while neglect can be both physical and emotional. Household dysfunction encompasses a volatile home environment that can result from a variety of factors: a family member or many family members who have a mental illness such as depression, anxiety, or PTSD, a family member enduring physical or emotional abuse (i.e., a parent being beaten by a spouse or partner), a relative who has been incarcerated, divorce, and substance abuse/addiction (The Centers for Disease Control and Prevention, 2019; Robert Wood Johnson Foundation, 2013).

Child psychologist at Stanford University School of Medicine, Hilit Kletter, discussed the importance of looking out for red flags that can lead to early intervention for children who are victims of childhood trauma. "Some children may have nightmares or recurring thoughts of a stressful event or may re-enact the trauma through play. Others may seem distracted or withdrawn. This will come out at school", Kletter said. "Teachers will tell parents that their child seems to be in a daze in the classroom, not paying attention" (Starecheski, 2015).

It is essential not to ignore, dismiss, or minimize these behavioral changes when noticed. Today, knowledge of ACEs can lead to early prevention and detection of childhood abuse and trauma for millions of children globally. Getting to the root of abuse in a way that identifies harmful behavioral patterns has been Dr. Harris' focus as she treats children who are victims of childhood trauma. Her expertise has shown that adults who physically, mentally, and sexually abuse their children often admit to having an overactive stress response stemming from their own early adverse life experiences. Dr. Harris believes that raising awareness takes precedence over separating families and incarcerating them. When the public is armed with facts and knowledge about the signs of childhood trauma, solutions can be offered that break the cycle of adverse behaviors before it becomes normalized and habitual. "We are on a mission to interrupt the transmission of the generational patterns of abuse with information and replace it with nurturing responses which release large, natural amounts of oxytocin," noted Dr. Harris (Harris, 2014).

THE IMPACT OF ACES

The higher the ACE score, the greater the risk for adult health problems. Adults with high ACE results are more likely to engage in unhealthy behaviors such as smoking and abusing alcohol and other drugs. They also might display apathy toward their jobs as evidenced by frequent absences and are less likely to develop a healthy exercise routine. The weight of adults who have suffered through childhood trauma has been observed on two extremes: dangerously skinny and morbidly obese. Typical physical and mental health issues observed in those with high ACE scores include diabetes, heart disease, cancer, strokes, COPD, STIs, osteoporosis, depression, and suicidal thoughts and behaviors.

Sadly, many adults who had suffered through childhood trauma were misdiagnosed during adolescence with learning disabilities, as much of the research on how trauma impacts learning is relatively recent. Developmental needs might not have been met in the classroom, and these same adults might have received a special education diagnosis during their formative years. For example, child psychologist Kletter states that it is common for children who have been victims of trauma to be misdiagnosed with attention deficit hyperactivity disorder (ADHD) because children with high ACE scores tend to act out of anger and impulsivity as a response to their trauma (Starecheski, 2015). Many behaviors typical of an ADHD diagnosis may be, in fact, the body's natural reactions to adverse or traumatic circumstances. For example, if we see a bear coming toward us, the amygdala, our body's fear center, would be alerted. When children have been repeatedly abused, stress hormones such as cortisol are continuously released with adrenaline to anticipate the next traumatic event. At this point, neurons in the brain begin firing off, and the child unknowingly goes into three states: "fight," "flight," or "freeze."

Dr. Jack P. Shonkoff, a professor of Child Health and Development at the Harvard T.H. Chan School of Public Health, has researched testing interventions that foster resilience in children growing up in adverse conditions that stem from poverty or chronic stress brought on by racial and gender discrimination. Dr. Shonkoff's work has been credited for equipping children from adverse conditions with the tools to excel academically, and it was his research that concluded that just one caring, safe relationship can be the contributing factor to a long, healthy life as an adult (Harvard Graduate School of Education, 2020).

The health implications surrounding high ACE scores reiterate the importance of external support networks such as schools and community-based organizations to facilitate recovery from childhood trauma. One voice of affirmation, love, and support can save lives when approaching childhood abuse. Preventing ACEs has the potential of reducing depression in adults by 44%. By preventing high ACE numbers, several health conditions could be reduced dramatically. Specifically, there are up to 21 million cases of depression, nearly 2 million cases of heart disease, and roughly 2.5 million cases of obesity in the country. By attending to the ACE assessment results, our planet could be a healthier home than it currently reports (Center for Disease Control and Prevention, 2019). Dr. Harris' call to action regarding preventative care of the potential health issues that stem from childhood trauma is underscored by the $3.8 trillion spent annually on health care, 90% of which goes toward fighting chronic diseases (Center for Disease Control and Prevention, 2021).

"What makes me really sad is why we are not spending this money on prevention techniques before it's too late," Dr. Harris discussed. "Heart disease is the number one killer in America, and survivors who have four or more adverse childhood experiences are twice as likely to have heart disease." She reiterates that the information correlating ACEs to long-term chronic illnesses is accessible despite rarely being considered when formulating treatment plans for combating chronic diseases. Dr. Harris further postulates that if ACEs are appropriately utilized, early intervention techniques could significantly reduce addictive behaviors such as drug and alcohol use, often used to relieve the adverse effects of childhood trauma. "If we identify early and get help early, we can change the odds in favor of a healthy, productive future for victims and the abusers" (Harris, 2014).

HOW ARE ACES CONNECTED TO HUMAN TRAFFICKING?

Research has shown a direct correlation between high ACE scores and human trafficking. According to a 2009 literature review, the following ACE indicators contributed to children becoming more susceptible to minor domestic sex trafficking: sexual/physical abuse, substance abuse by a family member, loss of a parent or caregiver, lack of support systems, and physical/emotional rejection from a parent or caregiver (Clawson et al., 2009). In the state of Florida alone, 913 male and female juveniles who accessed the trafficking hotline between 2009 and 2015 all presented with the following two ACE indicators: physical/emotional rejection from an adult caregiver and childhood sexual abuse. According to a U.S. National Library of Medicine report, male and female juveniles who had a history of previous sexual abuse were 8.2 and 2.5 times more likely to be trafficked, respectively (Reid et al., 2017).

In a 2002 study by Norton-Hawk that observed 106 Boston women who had either been or were currently incarcerated for prostitution, 68% of the women reported being sexually abused before the age of 10, and almost half reported being raped before the age of 10 (Norton-Hawk, 2002). In a 2001 study commissioned by the Center for Impact Research, 222 women currently engaged in prostitution in the Chicago region were studied, and 83% reported growing up in a household where addiction was present. ACEs such as abuse and addiction have the potential to put a young child on a collision course with human trafficking (Clawson et al., 2009).

The epidemic of human trafficking is sadly a global one, and other ACEs such as death and abandonment can place a child at further risk of being trafficked. A 2002 Canadian study by Nixon, Tutty, Downe, Gorkoff, & Ursel observed 47 women engaging in sex work and found that 64% of the women had been in the child welfare system, 78% of whom had entered the foster care system or lived in group homes (Nixon et al., 2002).

When nurses and other medical professionals properly gather information detected from the ACE checklist, there's the potential for human trafficking to be averted. As the research mentioned above has shown, the ACE checklist can identify potential victims of human trafficking. If a child scores higher than 6 out of 10 ACE indicators, they are more likely to become victims of human trafficking (Reid et al., 2017). Uninformed responses such as, "Why didn't they just leave their trafficker," fail to consider how powerful the bonds of trauma can be. Many victims of human trafficking have high ACE scores due to their repeated exposure to trauma in childhood. As the studies above indicated, many women who were sex trafficked had childhoods in which sexual abuse, addiction, and substance abuse were present. According to Estes and Weiner, the average age of sex trafficking for boys and transgender youth is 11, and the same study also confirmed that 25 to 35% of boys who had been sex trafficked were sexual and gender minorities (i.e., LGBTQ or gender-nonconforming) (Estes & Weiner, 2001). A 2006 study by McKnight confirmed that many young men and boys who had been trafficked were forced out of their homes due to their sexual orientation (McKnight, 2006).

Children and youth who experience the traumas of homelessness, food, or housing instability are at a greater risk of being victimized by sex traffickers. A 2006 study by Martinez found that sex traffickers target homeless youth because they are keenly aware of their need to survive. When adolescents have no idea when their next meal will be or where they will sleep for the night, they are sadly forced into situations where they can be taken advantage of by individuals who prey on their vulnerabilities.

According to a webinar produced by the National Center for Campus Public Safety, the recruiting grounds for trafficking candidates are many: bus stops, train stations, subway systems, shelters, concerts, shopping malls, juvenile detention centers, group foster care homes, youth events, schools (by word of mouth from student to student), courthouses, and colleges and universities. (Juneau & Banta, 2018).

Additionally, individuals who fall into the following four categories are also high-risk for trafficking. Undocumented immigrants often fall victim to sex trafficking for many reasons, one of which is that they often fear government agencies such as the Department of Homeland Security (DHS) or the police and, as such, fail to report abuse to police for fear of deportation or arrest. Some victims have been scared into silence by family members who pressured them into commercial sex work. When a victim fears homelessness, loss of food/water, and loss of clothing for their entire family, they feel the intense pressure to keep engaging in commercial sex work as a means for survival. Those who do not think they are victims comprise the third category. These victims have been brainwashed by the perpetrators who have terrorized them to the point that they become fearful of others and isolated from any existing support system. Trauma bonds are often prevalent between these victims and perpetrators, and it is common for victims to feel like a hostage to the captor who expresses occasional sympathy and intimacy. Victims who have been involved in the criminal justice system also face additional risk factors for trafficking. Many have endured abuse in childhood and use defense mechanisms such as defiance, disrespect, and aggression to protect themselves from further abuse. A common thread among these victims is trauma and the subsequent mental health challenges resulting from that trauma. When trauma has not been adequately addressed and treated, it can create a perfect storm for traffickers to lure and capture victims into both labor and sex trafficking (Interpol, n.d.).

NURTURE OVER NATURE

Dr. Harris's research has proven that "nurture over nature" can override the epigenetic markers of trauma and even change DNA, proving that changing one's environment can effectively treat trauma. In the animal kingdom, better executive functioning has been observed in families where nurture and support exist. For example, when a puppy rejected by its biological family was placed with a different female dog who nurtured it, the puppy's epigenetic markers changed when it was away from its birth mother. Science has undoubtedly proven that love, nurture, and support can change the structure of our DNA (Harris, 2014). All the survivor stories in Part One show how nurture can be one antidote to a toxic upbringing filled with abuse and neglect. Despite being subjected to years of sexual, physical, and emotional abuse, all the survivors have consistently worked on healing from their childhood trauma, rising above their circumstances, and not allowing their trauma to define them.

CHAPTER NINE
WOLF IN SHEEP'S CLOTHING

Imagine being five years old and finding yourself in a harrowing world of addiction, family dysfunction, incarceration, and sexual violence. This was Hadley's reality, which is sadly one that far too many children face. Hadley's support system was shattered after her parents' bitter divorce, leaving her mother with full custody of Hadley and her siblings as her father served a jail sentence on drug charges. Her mother struggled to remain employed, and there were long periods of financial instability for the family. Amidst the chaos, a 64-year-old man named Jake came into Hadley's life under the guise of wanting to help her family stay together and get back on their feet. At the time, Hadley's mother saw this man as the answer to her prayers and welcomed his help as her overdue bills and unpaid rent piled up.

Jake had offered to step in and help the family with their housing concerns, something Hadley's mother was grateful for as she believed that she and her children were one more missed rent payment away from homelessness. Jake owned several rental properties, one of which was a building that housed a childcare facility. The fact that this building was a mere two blocks away from Jake's home did not raise any concerns at the time, and Hadley's mother had graciously accepted Jake's offer to take her and her children to church with him. At the time, Hadley's mother had believed that Jake was just a good person who wanted to embody the teachings of his faith by helping others in need. She didn't realize Jake's acts of "kindness," such as taking the family to church with him on Sunday morning, were grooming techniques he deliberately employed to win her trust.

As the months passed, Jake became a regular presence in Hadley's life. He would pick her up from preschool when her mother was working and buy her little trinkets and dolls. Knowing how tired Hadley's mother would be once she got home from work, Jake routinely took the family out to dinner. He became part of the family and attended school events to support the children. However, these dinners and gifts had a price, and sadly Hadley would be the one to pay it. Jake conspired to spend more time alone with Hadley, and this alone time resulted in hugging, kissing, and inappropriate touching.

Hadley's breaking point came in the first grade when she began sobbing uncontrollably to her mother after one of Jake's visits. Tearfully, she revealed to her mother that her "Uncle" Jake had been touching her inappropriately when he was babysitting her. Hadley's mother angrily confronted Jake about his behavior, but he vehemently denied touching Hadley and convinced her mother that he would never do such a thing. Hadley's mother allowed Jake to continue watching her children, but she began keeping a closer eye on him. This watchful eye would prove life-saving one fall afternoon in 2019.

Jake had taken the family apple picking in his truck with a large, rectangular lift. A relaxing afternoon in nature quickly developed into a shattering revelation of Jake's sexual abuse toward Hadley. Hadley's mother had become uncomfortable with the fact that Jake only invited Hadley to ride in the cherry picker with him. As Hadley came down, she ran to her mother in tears, confessing to her that Jake had sexually violated her once again. Hadley had disclosed everything at that moment, sparing no details about how "Uncle" Jake had repeatedly abused her and even threatened to harm the family if she said anything. Hadley's mother knew her daughter was telling the truth and reported Jake to the police despite his desperate pleas for mercy.

Even though Jake continued to deny the abuse, Hadley's mother warned the other parents at school about Jake's predatory behavior, prompting other mothers to come forward with similar stories about Jake. Many in the community had been afraid to speak out against Jake's sexually abusive behavior toward young girls. During Jake's trial, his estranged adult daughter made an unexpected appearance in the courtroom and revealed that she had been a victim of her father's sexual abuse as a child. The testimony forced Jake to admit his guilt and acknowledge the pain and suffering he caused so many young, innocent girls.

Though justice had been served in this case, Hadley's family was forever changed by this trauma and will be working through the devastating effects of it for years. Hadley's mother provided a powerful victim impact statement at Jake's sentencing, which illuminates the magnitude of pain and suffering Jake caused Hadley and her family:

My name is ***, and I am the mother of the now 6-year-old victim in this case. I honestly dreaded coming here being in the same vicinity as you. I literally have so much anxiety at the moment that I feel like I could vomit. But I know that I needed to be here to speak for my daughter. She deserves to have her story told.

The goal of this statement is not only to tell my daughter's story but to give a clear and concise picture of what kind of predator we have in our presence today. This is a criminal who has no control over his impulses and cannot be trusted around children or vulnerable adults, for that matter.

Before I go into specifics, I want to talk about the impact this incident has had on my daughter. Because of you, my daughter has nightmares multiple times a week. The nightmares almost always consist of you coming to get her, to hurt her, or to get revenge because she told the truth about what you did to her. You are the demons and monsters in my child's nightmares! Because of you, my daughter is scared of men, and she questions their intentions regardless of what they are doing or who they are.

Because of you, my daughter cowers when she sees a work truck that has a "bucket." Because of you, my daughter has to deal with grown-up topics and emotions! Because of you, my daughter has been diagnosed with PTSD! My 6-year-old has PTSD!

Please explain to me how you can hurt another person so profoundly and yet only be facing a few months in jail? That doesn't seem like justice to me, especially since I have not seen one OUNCE of remorse from you! But honestly, there is no amount of jail time that is comparable to the pain that has been inflicted on my child simply for your perverted pleasure. Your perverted desires that you have proven you are UNABLE TO CONTROL.

You see, you had so little regard for anything but your perversion that you stooped so low as to use God himself as a way to earn my family's trust. You would bring Christian literature over to our home, subscribe my kids to Christian magazines, invite us to attend church with you, and you even had a discussion with us about the children you had sponsored in far-off countries. This kind of sick human uses the Lord as a manipulation tool to hurt the most innocent beings in the world.... a child!

So, your Honor, I'm going to direct the rest of this message to you because I need your help. You see, when my daughter asks me why this happened to her, I REFUSE to let her feel like this was all for nothing. I explain to her that sometimes God lets bad things happen to good people for the greater good of the world. I explained to her that because she was so brave, honest, smart, and strong, God chose her to be the one that finally stops this monster. I tell her that she was put through this terrible incident to help protect other children and give a voice to all the other children he hurt. And I firmly believe that there are, in fact, many other children that have been harmed!

This man is in his mid-70s. He committed this crime while I was just standing a few feet away. What kind of criminal commits such a brazen crime in plain sight? A criminal knows EXACTLY what they are doing because they have done it many times without getting caught. This man is strategic, plotting, and manipulative. He has no boundaries when it comes to the lengths he will take to satisfy his own needs. This man is the very definition of a sexual predator.

I'm asking the court to impose the maximum jail time on the table today. I'm asking this so I can go home and tell my daughter that because of her, this monster cannot hurt any more children! That her pain and suffering were not all for nothing, and she should feel proud, empowered, and in control because she stood up for what was right. I want her to always trust that doing the right thing and telling the truth will always yield positive results. Please help me close this chapter for my daughter on a successful note.

I appreciate the opportunity I was given to speak today. Thank you!
Mother of the Victim

• • • •

WHO ARE THE PERPETRATORS?

Thankfully, Hadley had advocates who could stop the abuse she had suffered at Jake's hands. Though our society does not often view law enforcement officials as agents of healing and recovery, they can be. Retired law enforcement official Corporal Alan Wilkett is one of those first responders dedicated to stopping the spread of sexual exploitation of minors. His work with The Human Trafficking Foundation and Bridging Freedom aims to raise awareness about human trafficking and enact federal, state, and local legislation to combat human trafficking in the United States. Throughout his 27 years working in law enforcement and recent retirement from the Pasco County Sheriff's Office, Corporal Wilkett has served his community through investigating and contributing to the investigation of major crimes, homicides, and crimes of child abuse and human trafficking. His mission is to inform the public that commercial sexual exploitation is not an issue only developing countries face but a worldwide epidemic that transcends socioeconomic status.

"There is no 'one-size-fits-all' perpetrator. The psychological profile of a sexual predator has no distinction in gender, demographics, economics, or education. They penetrate all walks of life," Corporal Wilkett reflects. Since many perpetrators like Jake hide in plain sight, gaining the trust of their victims and their families to begin the sexual abuse, how do communities stop sexual exploitation and sex trafficking? How do they spot those children and adolescents who are vulnerable to sexual exploitation?

Perpetrators like Jake are adept at discerning the family dynamics of their victims, gleaning salient information about economic, emotional, and interpersonal stressors a child is facing through seemingly innocuous questions.

Various typologies have been developed to help understand deviant sexual behavior. However, according to the FBI, classifying sexual offenders has been problematic (Simons, 2014). Research has shown that sexual offenders exhibit a wide variety of characteristics yet have similar clinical issues and traits; the degree to which these clinical issues are evident varies among offenders (Gannon, Terriere & Leader, 2012; Ward & Gannon, 2006). Typologies include child sexual abusers, pedophiles, rapists, and internet sexual offenders. Not all individuals who sexually assault children are pedophiles. Pedophilia consists of a sexual preference for children that may or may not lead to child sexual abuse (e.g., viewing child abuse images). In contrast, child sexual abuse involves sexual contact with a child that may or may not be due to pedophilia (Camilleri & Quinsey, 2008). Within each typology are subcategories such as intrafamilial or extrafamilial and differences between male and female offenders that make profiling deviant sexual behavior very complex.

Offenders with deviant sexual behavior emerge from all races and ethnic groups, socioeconomic backgrounds, and diverse occupations and geographic locations. They can be parents, grandparents, aunts, uncles, friends, or strangers. If they are not family members, they often attempt to gain access to children by befriending parents, particularly single parents, offering babysitting services, becoming a guardian or foster parent, volunteering, chaperoning overnight trips, or loitering in places frequented by children (i.e., playgrounds, schools, parks, malls, sporting fields, and game arcades).

Offenders who also have a diagnosis of psychopathy are reported to lack empathy, guilt, or remorse and have a grandiose sense of self-importance. They are experts in reading people and playing to their vulnerabilities. Most psychopaths are prone to thrill-seeking and have a low tolerance for frustration. Studies report that it is nearly impossible for this kind of offender to be fully rehabilitated (Oxford University Press, 2013).

Offenders target vulnerable families. Those who seduce children often study and befriend a child first, promoting physical contact like wrestling, tickling, kissing, massaging, lap sitting, and back rubs. They often also test the child's ability to keep secrets and continually expose their victims to sexual jokes and pornography (Pennsylvania Coalition Against Rape, n.d.).

PREDATORS' GOALS AND BEHAVIORAL PHASES

Predators often exhibit five distinct behavioral phases. The initial tactic of many of these predators is to identify a potential victim. It is reported that there is a heightened level of danger when a predator is non-preferential in choosing a victim, confirming their desperate desire to access a child. Secondly, many predators then gather information about the child: Are they regular social media users? What are the child's likes and dislikes? Are they vulnerable and easily manipulated? Stage one and two do not pertain to predators who already have access to a child, reiterating the research that suggests in most cases of sexual exploitation, the perpetrator is someone the child knows and trusts, like a family member or close friend of the family, not a stranger (YWCA, 2017). Stage three includes identifying a need and being intent on filling it, as evidenced in Hadley's story when Uncle Jake ran to her mother to rescue them from debt after a brutal divorce. Typical to this stage is jealousy. Although Hadley's story did not occur online, there are some predatory similarities between these types of crimes. Uncle Jake became highly possessive of Hadley's friendships outside of his control. In the fourth stage, the predator shows desensitization and sexualization while enhancing intimate, sexual acts with the victim, sometimes including exposure to sexually graphic material. Stage five is when the perpetrator initiates the abuse. There is a sense of thrill exhibited for "getting away with it," as in the situation with Uncle Jake, who exploited Hadley in the lift box of a cherry picker in the direct presence of the mother (Maryland Coalition Against Sexual Assault, 2016).

At this point, many perpetrators attempt to pursue new victims to exploit. Predators are grossly manipulative, and those who don't have access to children intentionally target communities and institutions that provide open access to children (Child Abuse Watch, n.d.). For example, our activity center became an easy target for offenders in the initial years of establishing a place for kids to roller skate and hang out together. Any institution that works with or serves families in need should be aware that families where children suffer from a lack of bonding, supervision, or boundaries, can be high-risk homes (Child Abuse Watch, n.d).

In the words of Corporal Alan Wilkett, "sex predators are in constant search of the places where children congregate. In times past, bus stations, parks, playgrounds, malls, and theaters were their haunts. Today, the predator is adapting to the new gathering places on online platforms such as social media, apps, and gaming systems, as confirmed by Corporal Alan Wilkett. Online predators collect and trade child abuse images. While some are content with possessing these images for their gratification, most seek to lure the child into a face-to-face encounter to complete their fantasy and deviant appetite. The online predator seeks anonymity and easily cloaks themselves with a fake profile specifically designed to build relationships with the potential victim. The predator's intentions are a sexual encounter. It is not unusual to have an adult perpetrator masquerade as a teenager to build an online relationship and convince the minor to meet them."

Corporal Wilkett went on to share that "once trust has been built between a victim and predator, "sextortion" begins. This is a grooming process where gradually sexual content is introduced into the conversation. The child receives more and more graphically explicit directions and demands from the predator, often forcing the child to self-produce child abuse images. The predator will manipulate the victim using fear tactics and shaming techniques into continuing the sexual relationship by threatening to expose the child abuse images, texts, or acts to their parents, family, friends, etc. The game is all about control and manipulation."

CHAPTER TEN
IF MY SUSPICION IS CORRECT

How does a bright, inquisitive, and talented young girl become withdrawn and disengaged in school? What was going on at home that made her arrive at school late, malnourished, and sleep-deprived? These had been questions I asked myself when trying to figure out how to reach Kelsea, a student of mine whose love of learning had inexplicably disappeared without warning.

When children suffer through complex traumas, they will often communicate their experiences in a way that feels safe for them. I had started noticing changes in Kelsea's behavior in class. She would appear sullen, withdrawn, and completely disengaged from the lesson. As is typical for teachers, I would walk around the room to observe the students' work, answer questions, or check to ensure they were staying on task. While other students were engaged in their lessons, Kelsea would draw pictures of a mature nature in the margins of her notepad. I would find her illustrating images of snakes, ashtrays containing a half-smoked cigarette, images of the naked body, and numerous romantic themes that appeared to me to be much too mature for an 11-year-old girl. These drawings provided me with a window into Kelsea's thoughts which caused me to pay closer attention and follow up with other school staff.

I had initially thought Kelsea was just slacking off when she did not complete her homework or participate in class. However, her frequent absences and her family's lack of involvement in school activities led me to suspect something else was happening. The adult-themed drawings in the margins of her notebook further concerned me.

I discovered a school counselor had also been alerted by Kelsea's frequent absences and disengagement from school. After adequately reporting my concerns as a mandated reporter, a home visit confirmed that Kelsea had suffered multiple sexual assaults. In addition to her sexual abuse, she witnessed her mother's drug use and was left at home with her mother's boyfriend. As a result of her mother's addiction, she lost her job and left Kelsea behind as she went to her sister's home two states away for support. With only her mother's abusive boyfriend around to watch her, Kelsea was repeatedly victimized. As a result of adequately reporting the suspected abuse, Kelsea was able to get the help she needed.

Kelsea's priority had been surviving the heinous abuse at home, so schoolwork was the last thing on her mind. My mission and challenge as a classroom teacher were to figure out how to create feelings of validation in Kelsea while helping her accomplish her schoolwork. Naturally, my first response was to attend to Kelsea's physical needs before expecting her to engage academically. I had to fully comprehend how a young girl in the throes of surviving neglect and sexual exploitation might struggle to complete a social studies term paper. Knowing that Kelsea had started the year off with an impressive amount of motivation to achieve allowed me to see her potential. Once she was in a safe home environment, she was better positioned to thrive in school.

HOW TO RECOGNIZE THE WARNING SIGNS AND RED FLAGS

Protecting our children by identifying a child victim of a sex crime, correctly reporting, and advocating for them to get the services they require certainly takes a network of people. As adults who work with youth, we are mandated reporters. We all have a responsibility to do our part. No one can do it alone. Educators can't. Law enforcement can't. Child Protective Services can't. Health Professionals can't. Mental Health professionals can't. Prosecutors can't. But together, we can tackle the horrific epidemic our children face.

Nurses are often the first contact for children and adolescents in distress. Children and adolescents often communicate their abuse in subtle ways, and school nurses are trained to look for the subtleties in these behaviors. As an ER trauma and school nurse with over two decades of experience, Jennifer Wolff shares firsthand how trauma presents itself in children and adolescents and how, as we saw in a previous chapter, specific adverse childhood experiences or ACEs increase an individual's risk of being further abused and trafficked.

Wolff shares that "if there is anything that I have learned while working in the school system as a nurse, collaboration between teachers and school nurses assure students are operating at their physical and mental best. Teachers are with their students the majority of the day, and they know them best. They know when a student is just having an off day, or something is not quite right. Typically, teachers send students to the clinic for an evaluation which can reveal red flags of something deeper going on. With over twenty years of emergency experience in ER medicine, I have no difficulty assessing a student's physical symptoms. But in many cases, the student may exhibit very vague symptoms that require me to circle back to other colleagues to hear their observations that prompted their initial concern."

As documented in a position paper published by the National Association of School Nurses, school nurses take on the roles of health detectives as they look past benign complaints of common ailments like stomach aches to get to the root causes, which are often found to be issues at home, depression, or stress at school (NPR, 2016; National Association of School Nurses, 2018).

In a recent article from Science Daily, one researcher stated that there is a fair amount of anxiety in our teenage population, most of which goes untreated. Dr. Rebecca Bitsko confirmed that the number of children diagnosed with anxiety has increased over the years, with a 2011-12 survey showing 5.3% of children and teens being treated for anxiety. Despite the upward tick in treatment for anxiety, nearly 20% of children and teens who suffer from depression or anxiety did not receive the treatment for these conditions for an entire year. "About 70% of my day-to-day work is anxiety related. It usually starts with general somatic complaints and stomach aches. Anxiety is a big one related to stress for a variety of reasons," Wolff confirmed. This is also true for the children Ms. Wolff regularly treats as a school nurse. She reports, "On any given day, at least half if not more of the students I see have somatic complaints that when investigated further the students admit could be the result of an underlying factor that is creating anxiety" (Wolters Kluwer Health, 2018). According to a 2018 study in the Journal of Developmental and Behavioral Pediatrics, the number of American children diagnosed with anxiety or depression has risen from 2.6 million in 2012 to nearly 15 million in 2018 (Rosenfeld, 2018; Bitsko et al., 2018).

A red flag of sexual exploitation that nurses, healthcare, and educational professionals should be aware of is the student who continues to arrive at the school clinic with vague complaints. In many cases, students who continue to present with somatic complaints like headaches, stomach pains, and fatigue yet have no objective signs of illness need to be investigated further. Frequenting the school clinic is a red flag that the student struggles with something they want to talk about but don't know how to ask for help. Another red flag is persistent anxiety due to relationship issues, bullying, family issues, and of course, abuse. At its worst, anxiety can present as insubordination, hyper-vigilance, fearful demeanor, and panic attacks (Child Welfare Information Gateway, 2019).

Behaviors that can raise red flags of commercial sexual exploitation are defensiveness, violent peer interactions, lack of eye contact, depression, self-harm, hypersexuality, suicidal ideation or behavior, and class absenteeism, a common factor seen in sex-trafficked students. Physical marks such as tattoos or other noticeable markings could indicate ownership by a trafficker. A major red flag is if a student refuses to relinquish control of their cellphone, which suggests that the trafficker could be communicating with the student (Child Welfare Information Gateway, 2017).

"Sexual exploitation is no discriminator of age, and one of the biggest challenges for a school nurse is weeding through the symptoms students present and getting to the root cause of the issue," Wolff states. She identifies risk factors she terms "push factors" that place adolescents at risk of commercial sexual exploitation. These push factors, including family instability, a history of familial abuse, lack of overall supervision, lack of supervision of social media accounts and internet usage, and time spent in foster care or child welfare services, mirror the ACEs mentioned in this chapter.

Wolff notes that the common thread among these "push factors" is vulnerability. Sexual predators prey on the vulnerabilities of their victims and exploit them for personal gain. Therefore, it is imperative for teachers, school nurses, and all medical and educational professionals to learn about the subtle ways in which children and adolescents disclose the abuse they are suffering. While the school nurse may be the first point of contact for an abused child, they will often consult with teachers, guidance counselors, and other school officials to obtain all the necessary information to intervene on behalf of the abused child or adolescent.

"Remember that during your interaction with students, if their basic needs are not being met, like food and physical safety, there's no way to get them any higher in the triage [of Maslow's hierarchy of needs]," Wolff asserts. Many children and adolescents who have been sexually exploited are merely struggling to survive daily. Unless their needs are met, they will be reticent about their abuse.

When children operate in survival mode, it is essential to understand that they have often been subjected to years of abuse, neglect, and trauma. Articulating the details of their abuse might be a monumental task, as the abuse could have occurred over several years or could still be occurring. An understanding of Adverse Childhood Experiences (ACEs) provides "first responders" (teachers, nurses, doctors, teachers/school administrators, and law enforcement officials) with the types of trauma children experience and the health implications as a result of that trauma.

Many children being sexually exploited commercially have a history of childhood sexual abuse and trauma. Identifying the warning signs can help them receive the services they need before additional victimization occurs. In younger children, signs of abuse can include gradual or sudden behavioral changes, cruelty toward others and animals, persistent nightmares and disrupted sleep patterns, unusual/unhealthy curiosity in or knowledge of sex, fear or avoidance of a particular person, and loss of interest in friends, school sports, or other activities they once found enjoyable (Ivie, 2020). Red flags predominant in older children can include volatile outbursts of anger without provocation, running away, feelings of worthlessness, self-destructive behavior such as self-mutilation and substance abuse, promiscuity, eating and anxiety disorders, suicidal thoughts or actions, and signs of post-traumatic stress disorder (PTSD) (Ivie, 2020; Stop It Now, 2008).

It has been established early in this text that had the contributing survivors had the opportunity to have red flags identified in their early years, the trauma they continued to endure very likely would have been lessened. As a special alert to parents, youth workers, and especially teachers, the following warning signs are prevalent among children who are being sexually exploited: (1) withdrawal from family and school activities; (2) erratic display of mood and jumpy, nervous, or unpredictable outbursts; (3) decline in grades; (4) trouble sleeping; (5) sudden reluctance to use a computer and other electronic devices; (6) quick departure from or closing of a computer screen when others enter the room, showing a secretive nature regarding their digital life; (7) an intense preoccupation with talk of self-harm or suicide; (8) drastic changes in appetite; (9) display of a wide range of emotions, including frequent anger, sadness, or depression; and (10) a decrease in self-esteem (Parents Protect, n.d.).

There are also some additional ways in which signs of sexual exploitation might show up in classroom spaces. Strosahl and Robinson (2015) outlined nine different ways students' anxiety might present itself through multiple defense mechanisms, which can help educators understand the minds of those who are hard to reach and teach. The "Busy Bee" avoids stress by staying busy at all costs. This student often takes on too much and feels overwhelmed with responsibility as a result. The "Butterfly" struggles with task completion and struggles to focus on a single task at a time. The "Ostrich" is an expert at avoidance and will quickly divert to another subject to avoid dealing with a current stressor. The "Twiddler" operates in a state of nervous frenzy and tends to zone out with repetitive motions, such as wringing their hands or twirling their hair. The "Rationalizer" is an expert at explaining away their stress through denial and rationalization. The "Busybody" fixates on what everyone around them is doing to divert attention away from themselves and their circumstances. The "Worrier" operates in a constant state of worry to be drawn away from the pain of personal stress. The "Stoic" bottles up emotion and works hard to keep signs of any stressor under tight control. And the "Dumpster" uses whatever means they can to numb out their pain, including using drugs, drinking, overeating, or sleeping excessively (Strosahl & Robinson, 2015).

It is crucial to approach each anxious type of behavior with sensitivity and care, especially if you suspect such behavior might be a trauma response and need to take steps to report the suspected abuse properly.

HOW TO PROPERLY REPORT

As sex crimes against children escalate in severity and number, it would be unwise and harmful for anyone who regularly interacts with, educates, and cares for children to not prepare for an instance in which a child discloses sexual abuse to them. An educator faced with a child who just revealed sexual abuse might be at a loss regarding how to handle the situation best or feel like they do not know how to respond appropriately. As mandatory reporters, the information below gives us a roadmap to respond to abuse in a trauma-informed manner while still adhering to proper state protocols.

The NAIS Handbook on Child Safety by Rizzuto and Crosson-Tower suggests guidelines an educator can utilize when responding to a child disclosing abuse. It is essential to use both trauma-informed verbal and non-verbal communication. The following suggestions will help ensure that educators respond in a trauma-informed manner (Rizzuto and Crosson-Tower, 2016).

- Find a safe and neutral space that limits interruptions.

- Sit at eye level with the child and give them your undivided attention

- Reassure the child and let them know you believe them (the number of false reports by children is negligible).

- A child might make you promise to keep what they shared with you a secret. Do not make any promises to the child, especially related to secrecy. If what the child shares is abuse or suspected abuse, you are legally required to make a report with Child Protective Services.

- Let the child share in their own words. Do not pressure the child for additional information. Do not ask leading questions. Do not interject.

- Do not interview the child. Document what the child says in writing, placing quotations around specific comments they shared with you after the conversation. Do not add or take anything away from what the child said.

- Respond calmly, even if the information the child tells you is challenging to hear. It is important not to respond with shock, disgust, or alarm.

- Do not make judgmental comments about the abuser. Abusers are often someone who has formed a bond with the child.

- Reassure the child that they are not at fault.

- If the child shares information regarding a person the child lives with or will have contact with after school, consider the situation an emergency, and handle it immediately by contacting Child Protective Services (CPS) and local law enforcement. law enforcement will often respond to the call quicker than CPS.

- Ensure confidentiality by only seeking support from your supervisor and appropriate school counselor, school nurse, and resource officer. The child's privacy must be protected.

- Explain to the child that you must tell someone else to help them. Let the child know that someone else will probably need to talk with them, but they will be a safe person to talk to.

- Assure the child that you or another designated school staff member will be available for support whenever possible. Keep your word. If you say it, follow through.

- Remember that children who disclose abuse are often frightened or anxious and need additional encouragement and support.

- Do not confront the abuser. This may cause more harm to the child.

- Report the abuse to Child Protective Services. Visit www.childwelfare.gov/organizations to locate your state child abuse reporting numbers.

Any child who has been sexually exploited requires a network of reliable and reputable agencies and organizations to protect and support them.

It is unrealistic to expect one person to meet all the needs of a child who has disclosed abuse. It is vital to properly report suspected child abuse to access the help and resources they deserve. Educators play an essential role, as does everyone in the support network, including the CPS team, law enforcement officers, child advocacy centers, mental health professionals, health professionals, prosecutors, etc. It is easy to feel alone or overwhelmed when working with a child who has survived abuse. Remember, no one can or should do it alone!

Rizzuto and Crosson-Tower further explain that "although all states require suspected abuse to be reported, no state requires that the reporter have conclusive proof that the abuse or neglect occurred. Educators are not expected to be investigators. The law clearly states that reports must be made when abuse is observed, the educator "suspects," or "has reasonable cause to believe" that a child has been or is being harmed. In all cases, incidents must be reported as soon as they are noticed. Waiting for concrete evidence may put a child at further risk. When in doubt, report!" (Rizzuto and Crosson-Tower, 2016).

As Jennifer Wolff discussed earlier, nurses and other advocates often become like detectives when discerning whether or not a young person has been sexually exploited. She provides several risk factors to watch out for when intervening with suspected abuse or commercial sexual exploitation, detailed in the following paragraphs. She also agrees that the above bullet points outlining how to engage with a child disclosing abuse work for nurses, educators, and other advocates.

The risk factors for children being commercially sexually exploited or labor trafficked are separated into three criteria. The first criteria are designated for children who meet at least one of the following risk factors:

- A child exhibits behaviors or indicates either verbally or nonverbally that they are being controlled or groomed by an adult.

- A child spends significant time with people who have a history of commercial sex work.

- A child's electronic device (i.e., cellphone, computer) or social media activity contains sexual content or social interactions atypical for their age.

The following recommended protocol should be followed in the first criteria when an adult suspects a child is being actively recruited or exploited for sexual or labor purposes.

- Step #1 – Submit a mandated report to Child Welfare Services if the above risk factors are present.

- Step #2 – Defer to local law enforcement, school resource officer, or school site administrator as they investigate potential threats of further harassment or exploitation and its impact on school safety.

- Step #3 – Provide school consequences, if applicable per EC Section 32282. Depending on the severity of the situation, law enforcement might make an arrest.

The second criteria apply to children who meet at least two of the following risk factors outlined below:

- A child has a history of running away from home or has experienced housing instability, including several foster homes or periods of homelessness, including "couch surfing."

- A child has had interactions with law enforcement or the juvenile justice system.

- A child has a history of truancy.

- Child's close relationships or friendships are of concern, placing them at risk of exploitation.

- A child has a history of substance abuse or addiction.

All of the risk factors identified are indicators that a child is a suspected victim of commercial sexual exploitation, and therefore have a more comprehensive protocol when responding to a suspected case of child commercial sexual exploitation. See below for the steps that should be taken:

- Step #1 – If you suspect a child is a victim of commercial sexual exploitation, immediately file a report with Child Welfare Services.
- Step #2 – Involve local authorities or SRO in the potential investigation.
- Step #3 – Investigate threats to school safety and potential opportunities for recruitment and harassment.
- Step #4 – If deemed safe and appropriate, and if the victim gives consent, consult with their parents/guardians about the victimization.
- Step #5 – Provide the victim and their parents/guardians with mental health or social services.
- Step #6 – If you are a counselor or social worker, periodically check in with the victim to see how they're doing and if they need any additional support.

If you suspect that a child is a victim of commercial sexual exploitation, implement the following protocol:

- Step #1 – Submit a detailed, mandated report with Child Welfare Services.
- Step #2 – Involve local authorities or SRO in the investigation.
- Step #3 – Investigate threats to school safety and potential opportunities for recruitment and harassment.

- Step #4 – Defer to local authorities for the investigation.

- Step #5 – If deemed safe and appropriate, and if the victim gives consent, consult with their parents/guardians about the victimization.

- Step #6 – Assess whether the child's current school placement is conducive to their situation. If not, make recommendations and arrangements for the child to be transferred to another school.

- Step #7 – Provide the victim and their parents/guardians with mental health or social services.

- Step #8 – If you are a counselor or social worker, periodically check in with the victim to see how they're doing and if they need any additional support (San Diego County Office of Education, n.d.).

Wolff is also a strong advocate for working cross-functionally with local law enforcement officials to help implement a standard protocol for intervention in child abuse cases when no such protocol exists. Most people are unaware that when abuse of a minor is suspected, state law requires that Child and Family Services be notified immediately. In Florida, for example, the Department of Children and Families manages the case and dictates the process for intervention. Wolff reiterates that schools need standard protocols for reporting child abuse, reflecting on how her experience as an ER nurse allowed her to see the importance of having a standardized protocol in place for reporting suspected child abuse and neglect.

"I quickly realized that we were seeing victims in the hospital setting, yet I knew for a fact they were falling through the cracks. We just weren't informed enough about what we were seeing in our patients," Wolff reflects on her time as an emergency room nurse. A recent study confirmed that 63% of human trafficking victims had been brought to the emergency room and that hospital staff is most likely the first point of contact for trafficked individuals (Mason, 2018). With jarring statistics such as this one, an opportunity arises for hospital staff members to become trained in identifying, treating, and providing the preventative care needed to ensure that victims of human trafficking do not return to their abusers (Mason, 2018; Lederer & Wetzel, 2014).

Wolff's realization that emergency room nurses, doctors, and other hospital staff members lacked the proper training to identify and treat sexually exploited and trafficked victims prompted her to investigate her hospital's policies regarding human trafficking. Though her hospital had a mandatory policy for reporting human trafficking, the policy had mirrored the existing domestic violence policy. It contained no information on the signs of human trafficking. She knew that she needed the buy-in and support from multiple departments. She began reaching out to the social work department to update the policy for treating human trafficking victims.

"We worked with a multidisciplinary group of nursing and social work faculty from our local university, with extensive experience in human trafficking, along with nursing students, the local state attorney's office, a local OB/GYN experienced in treating survivors, fellow nursing colleagues from my department, and a survivor/expert," Wolff reflects. She encourages school administrators to adopt a similar approach when creating policies for treating students who have been sexually exploited or trafficked (Schneider et al., 1995; Knox, 2020).

WHAT IF THE SEXUAL EXPLOITATION IS HAPPENING WITHIN THE SCHOOL?

"It is extremely disturbing for most educators to consider that a colleague might be abusing children, but it happens," notes Rizzuto and Crosson-Tower (2016). They go on to share that "a common response when a fellow educator is suspected of abuse, especially if that person is popular or a long-term employee, is to deny, rationalize, or ignore it. If a child reports that he or she is being sexually, physically, or emotionally abused by school personnel, school administrators should remember that it takes courage for an abused child to talk to someone." Remember that the number of false reports made by children is negligible. A child disclosing any form of abuse, including sexual exploitation, by school personnel or an administrator trusts the adult to whom they told, and the situation requires special attention (Rizzuto and Crosson-Tower, 2016).

After using the guidelines listed earlier to respond to a student disclosing abuse, the next step is to follow state law and contact Child Protective Services (CPS). You can also call your local law enforcement agency to report abuse after contacting CPS. CPS personnel will interview the child or refer the allegations to Law Enforcement (depending on the state's laws) to determine if the allegation is true and if the child knows of any other potential victims. If there are additional victims, the CPS investigator or Law Enforcement will interview other alleged victims. The situation should not be discussed with or among school staff (Rizzuto and Crosson-Tower, 2016).

The critical point to remember is that everyone must be a first responder to protect our children. The job of safeguarding our children from predators who seek to inflict harm is a never-ending one, and we all have a responsibility to remain vigilant and work together when addressing, reporting, and ultimately preventing crimes against children.

CHAPTER ELEVEN
NAVIGATING UNCHARTED WATERS

It was impossible for Sylvia, a young mother of six children, to stay in her first marriage due to her husband's controlling and abusive behavior. Safety for the children was her highest priority, and so she left one day as her husband was sleeping off a drunken stupor. Sylvia cleaned houses for a living. During the height of COVID-19, she was also employed by a local supermarket to deliver groceries to consumers who used internet shopping during the pandemic.

As a single parent working long hours six days a week to provide for her family, she had the additional task of assisting three of her school-age children with virtual school assignments. In desperation, Sylvia called upon her ex-husband to discipline their 14-year-old son and to help with his middle school assignments, for which she felt unqualified. A school laptop was on loan for the teen's virtual learning experience to continue. In three short months under the poor supervision of the father, Sylvia learned from the school counselor that her son was failing in all four core subject areas, had been caught for multiple acts of cyberbullying involving girls at his school, and had spent hours daily in front of the screen viewing pornography. Sadly, this scenario has played out in countless other homes where children are left with unsupervised access to electronic devices.

• • • •

PROTECTING CHILDREN FROM EVOLVING PREDATORS

Just as crimes against children have escalated, advocates have tirelessly worked to create awareness regarding how children are being sexually exploited and have lobbied to pass legislation that protects children. In 1984, after several tragedies, John and Revé Walsh and other child advocates founded the National Center for Missing & Exploited Children as a private, non-profit organization to serve as the national clearinghouse and provide a coordinated, national response to problems relating to missing and exploited children. Before organizations such as the National Center for Missing and Exploited Children (NCMEC), dialogue and legislation around sexual exploitation were non-existent. After the abduction and murder of the Walsh's son Adam, conversations about sexual exploitation focused on child abduction and stranger danger. As crimes against children evolved, advocating organizations worked hard to keep communities informed. Thanks to the ongoing work of child advocates such as the Walsh family, awareness and training campaigns related to sexual exploitation and legislative initiatives focused on protecting children have drastically improved. Although communities are better at identifying, reporting, and stopping sexual exploitation, these crimes remain significantly underreported. In addition, sexual predators are constantly inventing new ways to interact with vulnerable children to exploit them sexually.

Technology is one of the avenues predators utilize to meet and exploit vulnerable children. The internet has undoubtedly made safeguarding children from predators harder, and adults have to be vigilant when it comes to children's internet usage. As technology develops rapidly, so do online platforms utilized by children for educational and entertainment purposes. Although these platforms are created with good intentions, child predators are incredibly technologically savvy and know which websites, apps, and games to frequent when searching for victims. Educators, parents, and advocates aware of these potential dangers can implement strategies to help safeguard children. Designing practical ways to begin a meaningful dialogue with children regarding sex trafficking and exploitation is vital for such preventive measures. Since there are so many spaces online that expose children to possible sexual exploitation, adults must stay up to date with what is available to young people online.

Corporal Wilkett offers parents strategies to stop sexual predators from preying on vulnerable children and adolescents. The three stages of sex trafficking – recruiting, grooming, and trafficking – are moving heavily to online platforms. With the proliferation of social media, internet availability, and smartphone apps targeting children and adolescents, sexual predators have 24/7 access to the most vulnerable population. Sexual predators are adept at fabricating online identities and presences for the sole purpose of luring young people into an emotional relationship online. Essentially, teenagers can be groomed from their own homes thanks to the internet. Once a predator has gained the trust of a child or teenager, they begin crossing boundaries that slowly lead to sexual exploitation. Corporal Wilkett discusses how innocuous activities such as gaming are breeding grounds for sex trafficking. For example, there was one case where a teenager began conversing with a sexual predator through a gaming site, developing what they thought was a "close" relationship. This predator had convinced his teenage victim to meet face-to-face and immediately started sex trafficking them after that meeting.

To combat these technologically savvy predators, Corporal Wilkett suggests all parents should actively monitor their children's internet usage, enabling tracking features on their cell phones and placing parental controls on sites that traffickers visit (i.e., social networking sites and chat rooms). We learned during the global pandemic that even when much of the world went on lockdown, predators were not deterred by these quarantine orders.

They were in many instances emboldened when children started spending more time online for school and socialization, making them easier targets for predators. The dark web has also become an underground means of socialization in which sexual predators are encouraged to engage in sexual acts with minors. Competitions with rankings are commonplace, and predators "score points" when they engage in sexual acts that are more grotesque than their peers, bragging about their conquests in graphic detail in chat rooms (Cordua, 2019). This remains true post-pandemic as the reliance on digital communication has become more ingrained into the human psyche.

The National Center for Missing and Exploited Children's Cyber Tip Line reported receiving over 18.4 million reports in 2018, all of which involved some form of sexually exploiting children. These reports revealed pernicious acts of child sex trafficking, sexual exploitation, and rampant distribution of child abuse images while exposing the troubling ways sexual predators use the internet to groom children or teenagers for sexual exploitation. These alarming statistics make it crucial to engage our children in age-appropriate dialogue around internet safety and how sexual predators target children online. Once a child has been exposed to predatory behavior, the damage done to their mental and emotional health is devastating and can take years to undo (Owen, 2019, as cited in Ivie, 2020).

In a parental awareness video, Sgt. Wade Williams with the Collier County Sheriff's Office notes, "One of the worst things a parent can do is give their child an electronic device without any restrictions and without having a discussion with them about what they will encounter online." Parents don't want the predators to be the first person to teach their children through grooming techniques and exploit them. Suppose they do not take an active role in prevention. In that case, it is highly probable that eventually, these children will be exposed to harmful consequences, such as an online predator, cyberbullying, sextortion, or lewd content. (Ivie, 2020).

Corporal Wilkett acknowledges the inefficiencies in the criminal justice system when investigating a perpetrator. For example, a search warrant and subpoena can only be issued to a perpetrator once the investigating officer can develop probable cause. Then case-building requires the inspection of every suspicious file on an electronic device. Some devices can include up to two terabytes of child abuse images or other evidence, taking offices an average of 10 hours a day over two weeks to reach a conclusion. In the worst cases, the statute of limitations to prosecute the case has expired, and the perpetrator can keep preying on children. These onerous processes in the criminal justice system keep law enforcement officials several steps behind the perpetrator. With staffing shortages and financial constraints, the children suffer at the end of the day.

Though it might seem hopeless, Corporal Wilkett believes that there is hope if communities work together and communicate with one another. He is a witness to the power of teachers as advocates for children who have been abused and trafficked and recalls how a second-grade teacher saved the life of a little girl who had been sexually abused and trafficked by her uncles from the ages of four to eight.

"The first person who took the first step to help this innocent child was her second-grade teacher," Corporal Wilkett emotionally reflects. The teacher had noticed that the girl was not appropriately dressed for a winter day at school. Upon further observation, she saw that the girl was walking strangely and not wearing underwear under her skirt. Gently pulling the girl aside, the teacher sweetly asked if she was all right and if she wanted to talk about anything. When the girl responded that she was "too hurt to wear panties," this alerted the teacher to investigate the abuse this girl was suffering at the hands of her uncles. This teacher's protective instincts kicked in right away, and she began to ask the appropriate questions that would get law enforcement immediately working on behalf of this girl. With the help of a triage of advocates in law enforcement, child protective services, healthcare, and education, the child was removed from the dangerous environment in which she was sexually exploited and trafficked. Corporal Wilkett believes that advocates like this teacher exist within everyone. When communities prioritize the welfare and safety of children, they can stay steps ahead of perpetrators.

With the stakes for protecting our children so high, Corporal Wilkett approaches this arduous work of educating the community on how sexual predators lure children into sex trafficking as his life's assignment. "I feel called to the battlefield of violence and exploitation of other human beings who need an equal chance to thrive," he reflects, assigning himself the title "Warrior Poet" as he fights for the safety and welfare of our children. "As a warrior uses his shield for strength, defense, and protection, the soft poet loves the most broken and hurting," he notes. Bridging Freedom, a non-profit organization that serves runaways, homeless, and at-risk youth under the age of 18, seeks to provide safety, shelter, and wraparound services for young people who have been trafficked. "A large percentage of victims are lured into trafficking because they simply need a place to stay or food to eat," Corporal Wilkett remarks. Hopefully, cities around the entire world would operate with the same mission as Bridging Freedom, caring for those who have been abused in the most heinous of ways.

When we realize that many abusers are just as intelligent and technologically proficient as a cybersecurity professional, the urgency to protect the most vulnerable should be felt by every parent, teacher, nurse, doctor, and adult who contributes to the well-being of children and adolescents. No teenager would be sexually exploited or trafficked in a perfect world, but sadly we do not live in an ideal world. The least we all can do is work proactively to protect children from these predators and unconditionally support every child and adolescent who survives sexual exploitation and trafficking. No preventative measure is too small. That app a parent forbids their child from downloading or the tracking capability they activate on their child's smartphone might just be the thing protecting them from a devious adult looking for underage victims online. Conversely, there is no act of support too small for children and adolescents who have been sexually exploited. Simply creating a safe space at school, church, and home for survivors to open up about their trauma is an excellent start for fostering an atmosphere of support and compassion when addressing and discussing trauma around sexual exploitation and sexual violence.

TALKING TO CHILDREN ABOUT BODY SAFETY

If you are an educator or other advocate involved in educating parents with young children, it's important to help empower parents to discuss "safe" and "unsafe" touching with young children. A good example is teaching them that no one should touch them in any area that their bathing suit covers and that they should never touch anyone else in these areas or see pictures or movies that show these areas.

Use age-appropriate terms and phrases when discussing issues surrounding body safety. It is possible to discuss body safety without addressing sexuality. Young children can also be taught the difference between healthy and unhealthy secrets. For example, a surprise party is a healthy secret because its goal is to make people happy and informed at the right time, whereas secret touching is never appropriate. Teaching parents to develop open communication with children by creating judgment-free environments where they can speak freely and be vulnerable is an essential preventative measure.

It is also important that children use the proper names for their body parts. Young ones educated by their parents can identify their body parts using appropriate terms and explain the difference between safe and unsafe touch, a deterrent to a potential predator (Stop It Now, 2008).

The National Center for Missing and Exploited Children offers free age-appropriate resources on their website for educators to utilize in the classroom to teach children body safety, stranger danger, digital citizenship, and how to be safer on and offline. Visit our website resource page for the link to access these essential resources.

KEEP THE CONVERSATIONS ALIVE

It's important to encourage children to trust their instincts and ask questions when they don't understand the world around them. Open dialogue is critical where clarification and understanding are needed. When working with parents, help them find a topic taught in school and connect it to a current issue such as human trafficking. An appropriate example is slavery; a subject taught in school that children understand. Most of them believe slavery ended a century ago and can conceptualize why it is immoral for people to be enslaved. Discussions such as these are excellent opportunities to open the lines of communication and discuss the subject of human trafficking. It, too, is a slave industry.

According to the National Center for Missing and Exploited Children, stranger abductions are rare (National Center for Missing and Exploited Children, n.d.). About 115 children per year in the U.S. are victims of stranger kidnappings, with teenagers being the prime targets of strangers compared to younger children. This is why it is essential to teach children the difference between "good touch/bad touch." In most cases of sexual exploitation, the perpetrator is someone the child knows and trusts, like a family member or close friend of the family, not a stranger (YWCA, 2017). Despite this finding, advocates need to help equip parents to talk with their children about how to behave if approached by a stranger and trust their instincts if they believe something is wrong. Children should never be left unsupervised with unknown adults, and they should always travel in groups, as there is safety in numbers.

CHAPTER TWELVE
EVIDENCE-BASED CLINICAL SUPPORTS

How does the brain respond to unimaginable neglect, physical abuse, and sexual exploitation in heinous circumstances? What are the physiological processes that occur when we encounter traumatic events? Immediately, the limbic system is activated, and the stress hormone cortisol is released. The amygdala activates an automatic fight, flight, freeze, or fold response and the prefrontal cortex shuts down. Due to the brain's response, likely, a child will not recall all of the details of a sexual assault, such as the time it happened, the people in the house when the assault occurred, the exact sequence of events, the places the child was touched, and the duration of the assault (Thatcher, 2019).

The mind and the brain are distinctly different from one another. The brain is an actual, physical structure of bone, as seen in an MRI. Active neurons measured by an electroencephalogram generate the electricity flowing through them. Contrary to popular belief, the actual physical brain is not in direct contact with our biological mind. When our neurons are firing rapidly, we cannot slow them down (Philosophy Now, n.d.).

In moments of danger, the mind subconsciously assesses the situation and decides if it will react by facing, escaping, or hiding from danger. This involuntary response is referred to as fight, flight, or freeze. A person experiencing this response can feel extremely alert, agitated, confrontational, or have an overwhelming urgency to leave the location. A severe fight or flight response can become a panic attack and, in some cases, trigger an asthma attack in people with the condition (West, 2021).

Trauma affects two specific parts of the brain – the prefrontal cortex (the thinking brain) and the limbic system (the emotional brain). The prefrontal cortex is responsible for our choices, behaviors, personality, and sensory information processing, while the limbic system controls basic instincts, emotions, and the functions necessary for survival. In the context of trauma, emotions are typically unconscious physical sensations to threat or opportunity, which include a racing heart, a pit in the stomach, or tightening of the chest (Thatcher, 2019).

Often a traumatic experience becomes stuck in the emotional brain, and the event's details become detached from the reasoning center, the thinking brain. Those same trauma responses can be triggered by any situation leading to post-traumatic stress disorder (PTSD) and other mental health conditions (Hagan, 2019). For example, Merideth was sexually assaulted at eight years old by her father. It was not until she attended a lecture on sexual exploitation at the age of 44 that flashbacks flooded her memory of her childhood trauma. And though trauma fundamentally changes the brain's architecture, there is hope for recovery. Retraining the brain to think and act differently after abuse is a lifetime commitment, but if one is willing to do the work, one can live a healthy, productive life (Perina, 2017). Old mental tapes must be replaced with a new mindset (Pemberton & Loeb, 2020). Meredith's abuse left her isolated and in shame. She also lost all trust in her father and chose little to no involvement with her father when she was old enough to deal with her emotions. Many vulnerable survivors have difficulty coping with their emotions (limbic brain) because the rational brain is "stuck" in the past. "Healing comes when the rational brain moves into the present and sends the message that the abuser no longer has control of a survivor's life" (Hagan, 2019). Through the nudging of her therapist, Elizabeth went back to her childhood home and felt released from numerous haunting memories. She had remembered the house being much larger than it was. She expressed that there was something very empowering about going back to confront memories to attain a deeper level of healing.

While trauma is irreversible, there are resources and techniques to help survivors process it in healthy, constructive ways. The first and most crucial step is to point the survivor to resources to help them process their trauma safely. The survivor must be paired with the right resources because trauma can potentially change the developing brain's architecture (Palmieri & Valentine, 2021). Three highly successful methods used to help treat survivors are dialectical behavior therapy (DBT), cognitive-behavioral therapy (CBT), and Eye Movement Desensitization and Reprocessing (EMDR).

DIALECTICAL BEHAVIOR THERAPY

Therapy that centers on mindfulness has been proven effective in treating trauma survivors. A therapeutic practice that works well with a licensed mental health professional is Dialectical Behavioral Therapy (DBT). DBT is a vetted practice that begins to steer the brain into positive pathways to wholeness by using self-dialogue to interrupt negative thinking and create a positive mindset. It is recommended that those seeking therapy practice positive daily affirmations as part of their treatment. Statements such as "I am valuable, confident, and in charge of my emotions" and "I will rise above my current situation" are great mantras to recite daily (Schimelpfening, 2021).

Because the mind and brain are in two-way communications, the brain delivers the message to the mind through the senses of sight, smell, sound, and touch. In turn, the mind provides messages back to the brain that can help rewire it (Norman, 2016; American Association of Neurological Surgeons, 2021).

The primary function of the mind is to judge and control. It evaluates, compares, and predicts at record speed on an ongoing basis. Our brains are wired to make sense of the world. But when a survivor gets stuck in a critical mindset, thoughts of self-doubt or shame erupt, and an unhealthy stress response occurs unless we can intentionally rewire the messages we're sending to our brain (Schimelpfening, 2021).

Applying techniques learned in DBT helps understand how to tune out toxic narratives, be fully present in the moment, and focus on creating new positive thought patterns. Think of grooves or pathways in the mind that have been created by constant abusive dialogue. These grooves become the paths of least resistance for new thoughts, leading to survivors blaming themselves for the abuse. For example, survivors might think, "If only I wouldn't have worn the red dress, maybe Uncle James would not have attacked me," or "Maybe if I hadn't been so playful, my stepfather would not have pursued me." In actuality, the perpetrator's actions were not provoked by the survivor, but because the survivor had been brainwashed and conditioned, they assumed responsibility. In a crisis, we use the brain's advice to determine who we are, when in essence, we are much greater than the sum of our thoughts. When we lose the distinction between our thoughts and ourselves, this can cause great confusion, pain, and disconnection.

With DBT, survivors choose to listen to their thoughts or take another action that changes the message. Like a supercomputer, we can see the personal message on our screen and decide to read it or delete it (Schimelpfening, 2021). This takes considerable discipline, but the mind does not own your destiny; YOU do.

COGNITIVE BEHAVIORAL THERAPY (CBT)

It is critical to remember that genetics are not predestined. Even though our brains are genetically programmed to influence our behavior, behavior affects the brain. This is excellent news for trauma survivors because it means that explicitly through practice and cognitive-behavioral therapy

(CBT), survivors can often rise above their circumstances and not be defined by their traumatic experiences.

CBT is a solutions-oriented psychotherapeutic model designed to reduce emotional irregularities and return the patient to a sense of normalcy. It encompasses two main components – cognitive and behavioral. The cognitive element of CBT is geared toward changing patterns of thinking. The behavioral component is geared toward developing healthy behaviors and coping mechanisms to deal with stress and anxiety. This deliberate integration of feelings, thoughts, and behaviors into treatment makes this an effective model for those suffering from many mental health issues, including those resulting from the aftermath of trauma (Gillihan, 2018).

A case-in-point comes from a series of Stanford University studies that found that CBT fundamentally changes brain function, proving that the way the brain is wired does not seal one's fate to be permanently damaged and scarred after trauma. Imagine your brain bisected from one side to the other, ear to ear. On that line, behind your eyes, are two nuggets of neurons called the amygdala, which perform with great versatility. Dr. Ellen Hendrickson notes that "It's part of the eating system, sex system, addiction system, and while it's the only part of the brain responsible for handling fear, it is the lynchpin of the fear system. It receives sensory information. For example, the sight of a dog attacking someone or the sound of a bus heading straight for you start a reaction. The amygdala is our fire alarm designed to detect and respond to threats." Dr. Hendrikson notes that specific grounding techniques employed through CBT can help people react more effectively to various stressors (American Psychological Association, 2017).

Thoughts, emotions, and behaviors are closely interwoven in the brain and directly influence one another. CBT aims to change or intervene with one of these three domains to alter the other two, which can change the way someone thinks and, in turn, lead to greater overall wellness. When confronting tense situations, CBT can minimize the frequency of anxious thoughts (American Psychological Association, 2017).

Researcher, therapist, and author of the books *Retrain Your Brain* and *Cognitive Behavioral Therapy Made Simple*, Dr. Seth J. Gillian notes that patients undergoing CBT should consistently do the simple things such as engaging in enjoyable activities, thinking helpful thoughts, facing their fears, being present, and taking care of themselves. They should also understand the challenge of actively changing their thought patterns during periods of severe depression, motivation, and panic. It takes hard work to retrain thought processes, but CBT provides a systematic plan for handling seemingly uncontrollable and unmanageable emotions (Gillihan, 2016; Gillihan, 2018).

CBT's effectiveness in treating the mental health problems survivors of sexual exploitation face is due to its ability to break down personal challenges into manageable parts while retraining the brain to process issues in smaller, more realistic steps (Gillihan, 2018). For instance, when Elizabeth is triggered by a man invading her personal space, she uses grounding techniques, mindfulness to create new thoughts, and journaling to process her reactions after the incident. Instead of succumbing to the panic attacks brought on by recalling her father's invasion, she uses the techniques mentioned above to work through and manage her stress and anxiety. Though survivors of sexual exploitation can practice CBT to help address their mental health challenges, it is recommended that survivors work with a qualified psychologist, psychiatrist, or another medical professional as they process their trauma.

CBT can also be tailored for young children and adolescents. CBITS (Cognitive Behavioral Intervention for Trauma in Schools) is a school-based group and individual intervention for children and adolescents in grades 5 through 12 designed to reduce symptoms of PTSD, depression, and behavioral issues. Students who participate in this program have reported experiencing increased focus in the classroom and less stress (National

Child Traumatic Stress Network, 2012).

STRUCTURED PSYCHOTHERAPY FOR ADOLESCENTS RESPONDING TO CHRONIC STRESS (SPARCS)

SPARCS is a 16-session group intervention specifically designed to address the needs of chronically traumatized adolescents who may still be living with ongoing stress and may be experiencing problems in several areas of functioning. Due to trauma, many adolescents living with constant stress struggle with impulsivity, self-perception, interpersonal relationships, and finding meaning and purpose in life. This program aims to help teens cope more effectively, improve self-esteem, find community through establishing supportive relationships, and create meaning in their lives. Group members learn and practice each of the core SPARCS skills throughout the intervention and frequently report using these skills outside of the group (Complex Trauma Treatment Network, n.d.).

As CBITS and SPARCS have demonstrated, therapeutic interventions for children and adolescents who have suffered trauma can be effective. If a person is treated for their trauma earlier, they will significantly reduce the health risks associated with their respective trauma. Unfortunately, many of these therapies were not available decades ago. However, evidence-based therapies such as EMDR can facilitate healing for those who could not receive treatment for their trauma during childhood or adolescence.

EYE MOVEMENT DESENSITIZATION AND REPROCESSING (EMDR)

EMDR is a powerful new psychotherapy technique that has been highly successful in helping people who suffer from trauma, anxiety, panic, disturbing memories, PTSD, and other mental health issues. During trauma, the brain does not function properly. In one moment, it becomes frozen in time, recalling the images, sounds, smells, and feelings associated with the original trauma. EMDR therapy combines bilateral stimulation with right/ left eye movement in a way that activates the opposite sides of the brain, releasing emotional experiences that are trapped in the nervous system (EMDR Institute, n.d.).

ELIZABETH SHARES HER EXPERIENCE WITH EMDR

When I heard about EMDR, I was excited to try something new that could possibly rewire my brain from trauma and give me deeper relief in a shorter time. For those who have not experienced complex trauma, let me say that every day can be a constant reminder of horrific things you desperately wish you could erase from your memory. So, I was willing to try almost anything. My therapist, with whom I had a long-standing relationship, introduced EMDR into our sessions. We started small with some tapping exercises and then progressed into hand-eye activities. I was astonished by the progress. The tapping helped me with grounding techniques when I became overly anxious, and the hand-eye sessions relieved my complex PTSD. I will say, I had been in talk therapy for many years, so I felt I had already untangled many of my complex issues. EMDR came alongside my weekly therapy sessions and complimented them.

I have heard other survivors say their EMDR experiences uprooted their trauma and caused emotional discomfort, although that was not my experience. The difference-maker between my experience and theirs might have been due to the frequency of therapy sessions. These survivors were not in weekly sessions with a trusted therapist like I was. I found quick, significant results with EMDR as an addition to talk therapy. If we addressed an issue in EMDR, I never had to work on that specific issue again. After those sessions, I felt completely free from the negative emotions attached to that issue. It was as if my traumatic memories were stuck in my body, and through EMDR, my brain was able to reprocess them and let them go. I would highly recommend EMDR with a skilled therapist used in tandem with talk therapy.

• • • •

As the clinical supports outlined in this chapter have shown, there is hope for those who have undergone trauma. The critical takeaway here is to help connect young people and their families, if appropriate, with the professionals that can help them find the therapeutic techniques that work best. As trauma impacts people differently, so does therapy. A bad experience with a therapist or a particular treatment does not mean that someone should give up on treatment. Some survivors experience good results with individual and group therapy, while others thrive in individual or group therapy. Encourage survivors to keep an open mind and keep the lines of communication open with their therapist regarding progress.

CHAPTER THIRTEEN
ENVIRONMENTS OF HEALING

CREATING TRAUMA-INFORMED CLASSROOMS

Throughout *One Story, Many Voices*, we have read heroic stories from survivors who courageously shared their traumatic life experiences. These brave survivors selflessly shared the most horrific events of their lives, knowing they represent many others. According to the CDC, up to two-thirds of U.S. children have experienced at least one type of severe childhood trauma, such as abuse, neglect, natural disaster, or experiencing or witnessing domestic violence (Centers for Disease Control and Prevention, 2021).

RAINN, the Nation's largest anti-sexual violence organization, states that every nine minutes, child protective services either substantiates or uncovers concrete evidence of a claim of child sexual abuse (RAINN, n.d.). These statistics of violence and sex crimes against children in the United States are staggering and create awareness that many children will experience trauma at some point in their lives. Therefore, it is highly probable that educators, service providers, and health professionals will encounter a child who presents with traumatic stress symptoms. This naturally raises concerns in all of us as to how a well-meaning teacher, advocate, administrator, service provider, or first responder could potentially retraumatize a child without realizing it. How do we prevent retraumatization?

Before we can prevent retraumatization, we must first understand what trauma is. According to the U.S. Department of Health and Human Services Substance Abuse and Mental Health Services Administration or SAMHSA, trauma is an emotional response resulting from violence, abuse, neglect, war, loss, disaster, and other emotionally harmful experiences. It does not discriminate based on age, gender, socioeconomic status, race, ethnicity, geography, or sexual orientation. Even though many people who experience a traumatic event go on with their lives without lasting mental health challenges, others will have more difficulty and experience traumatic stress reactions (SAMHSA, 2014).

It is incumbent upon us as a society to work toward gaining a better understanding of how to address the trauma experienced by individuals to reduce retraumatization. As a result, there has been a renewed focus on the impact of trauma on individuals and how we can facilitate survivors in managing their traumatic stress reactions by operating with a trauma-informed approach (SAMHSA, 2014).

A trauma-informed approach starts with understanding the acute physical, social, and emotional impact of trauma on both the individual and the professionals who treat them. This approach then adopts survivor-centered techniques that incorporate three key elements: **realize** the prevalence of trauma, **recognize** trauma's impact on all individuals, and **respond** by putting this knowledge into practice and actively seeking to avoid retraumatization. It is vital to incorporate six fundamental principles to continue expanding on the three suggested elements: 1. Safety, 2. Trustworthiness and Transparency, 3. Peer Support, 4. Collaboration and Mutuality, 5. Empowerment, Voice and Choice, and 6. Culture, History, and Gender (SAMHSA, 2014). How do we ensure that our behavior aligns with our understanding of a trauma-informed approach? How do we create safe and supportive environments for individuals with traumatic stress symptoms?

"It's the little things," says Elizabeth. "Even though when I was in school, my teachers didn't have access to the trauma-informed training the way teachers today do, I do believe most of them did what they could to provide a nurturing and safe school space. It was in the way my kindergarten teacher encouraged me to find my voice through art while creating a safe Kindergarten classroom. The way my 5th grade teacher asked me to stay after school and help her organize. The way another teacher knelt down and looked at me as she gently spoke words of encouragement. When I close my eyes, I still see the ribbon she wore around her neck with the beautiful cameo attached. I would compare implementing a trauma-informed approach to creating a safe and nurturing space. It is a space free from dominating personalities that attempt to control every aspect of an outcome. It's a space where demands aren't made. It is a space where everyone can breathe easy because each person can be trusted. Don't we all crave a circle of mentors and friends that understand us, that we trust, and can work collaboratively on a project that has meaning? That type of environment gives birth to empowerment: finding one's voice. It gives us the courage to speak because we don't stand alone and are not afraid of being judged. It's a place where we accept and value one another no matter where we came from or what our stories are... isn't that a place we all dream of being a part of?"

A few tools that can easily be employed to implement a trauma-informed approach in the classroom, according to Jessica Minahan with ASCD, an organization empowering educators to achieve excellence, are to anticipate unexpected responses, employ thoughtful interactions, establish clear boundaries regarding relationship building, foster predictability, and consistency, teach and implement strategies to change the channel, provide supportive feedback to decrease negative thinking, create islands of competence, limit exclusionary behaviors, and foster feelings of safety. "Students can't learn if they don't feel safe," Minahan writes. Her article provides us with thoughtful questions below to help us apply these practices

(Minahan, 2019).

- What small changes are you willing to make in your classroom to foster a sense of safety among traumatized students?

- Reflect on one of your students who struggles with behavior. How could you help them "switch the channel" when they are upset?

- Do you routinely share and exchange ideas about how to work with traumatized students? How could you better improve lines of communication across the whole support team?

Classroom resources like the Sources of Strength (SOS) curriculum can also help schools, and classroom teachers, in particular, build up students' resilience and coping skills in the aftermath of trauma (Wyman et al., 2010). The mission of SOS is to provide the highest quality evidence-based prevention for suicide, violence, bullying, and substance abuse by training, supporting, and empowering peer leaders and caring adults to impact their world through the power of connection, hope, help, and strength. The Sources of Strength's vision states that many strengths are more powerful than one. Their united goal is to activate and mobilize these strengths in ways that positively change individuals and communities. The program details strengths that include mental health, family support, spirituality, medical access, mentoring, generosity, and healthy activities (Sources of Strength, n.d.).

Incorporating SOS principles into the kindergarten through 8th-grade curriculum has helped youth cope with adverse circumstances. Empirical studies on the SOS curriculum conclude that students will better handle unfavorable life circumstances if they exit 8th grade using three or four strengths. This program has been vetted in rural and urban districts and has been put into place as a preventative measure for youth struggling with suicide and other high-risk issues.

What is excellent about programs like the SOS program is that they teach children personal resilience, allowing them to use problem-solving skills to handle difficult situations. When managing stress, these principles are perfect for coping with the inevitable demands of everyday life in healthy, constructive ways.

• • • •

IDENTIFYING STRESS

Stress can be a primary contributing factor to depression because when the body becomes overwhelmed, feelings of anxiety and the desire to escape occur. While history and literature have provided ample evidence of the debilitating effects of stress going back centuries, scientific studies show that stress is a silent killer of many. Stress is directly related to the six most common causes of death: heart disease, cancer, cirrhosis of the liver, lung diseases, accidents, and suicide. Stress increases the chance of a heart attack later in life. And by weakening the immune system, stress not only makes us age more rapidly but also leaves us susceptible to numerous diseases (Kentuckyslone, 2019). Chronic stress is also connected to poor academic outcomes and a lack of social connectedness in young people.

The biochemical link between anxiety and depression is that an over-stressed brain is far more likely to become depressed. Anxiety usually presents itself first, followed by depression – a feeling of helplessness, often in the face of chronic conditions of anxiety.

One of the first steps we can take to help young people break the cycle of stress is to help them recognize when and where stress shows up in their lives. Here are some statements below that you can use with youth to help them identify their current stress levels. These statements work particularly well with adolescents and may need to be modified for use with younger children:

1. At the end of every day, I am exhausted.

2. Nearly every day, I feel completely rushed, even when I am on time.

3. My usual speed is "full throttle." I don't do slow well.

ONE STORY MANY VOICES

4. I tend to be distracted about what's going on in the future, and I miss out on today.

5. I prefer to function alone rather than with a group of people when I get home.

6. I often make sighing sounds.

7. Due to the pressure I put myself through, I do not take many needed breaks.

8. I have difficulty relaxing in my leisure time.

9. In my leisure, I find myself or others say I'm "zoned out."

10. I know exercise is good for me, but I have trouble motivating myself to do it.

11. I am in a constant mode of feeling "behind."

12. I often daydream when I am with my family and friends.

13. I am awakened in the middle of the night with tasks or thoughts on my mind.

14. I become impatient and irritable when I am under stress.

15. I feel guilty taking time for myself because, in my mind, that means I will be more behind.

If any of these resonate with the young people you're working with, it might help them honestly assess the toll that stress plays in their lives. Once the recognition is there, we can help them work through some best practices for relieving stress, especially the stress caused by the trauma they face or have faced in their lives.

Trauma-related stress often manifests itself through PTSD, which the following section describes in detail. As we saw in the survivor stories, an individual who has experienced repeated trauma in childhood can also begin experiencing PTSD symptoms in childhood and adolescence. It is critical for all first responders, whether a teacher, nurse, doctor, or school administrator, to identify the signs and symptoms of PTSD and other stress-related disorders and implement appropriate stress management techniques when possible.

TRAUMA AND OTHER STRESS-RELATED DISORDERS

Many people are exposed to varying degrees of trauma throughout their lives, such as losing a loved one, witnessing a horrific tragedy, or being physically abused or sexually exploited. Not all victims of trauma or abuse will be diagnosed with an ongoing condition, but trauma can result in various diagnoses, one of them being Post-Traumatic Stress Disorder (PTSD). PTSD is a mental health condition triggered by experiencing or enduring an extreme or life-threatening event. In most cases, the traumatic events that lead to PTSD include physical assault, physical abuse, sexual abuse, repeated exposure to violence such as military combat, a robbery or attack in which the victim is held at gunpoint, the witness of a violent assault or murder, terrorist attacks, natural disasters, near-fatal automobile accidents, mass shootings, kidnapping, and any circumstance that poses a threat to one's life (National Institute of Mental Health, 2020). Distressing feelings can follow a traumatic event for anywhere between a few weeks to a few months but subside over time. For others, however, these feelings persist longer than six months and can be an indicator of PTSD. Approximately 4% of U.S. adults have PTSD, and an estimated one in 11 will be diagnosed with it at some stage in their lives (American Psychiatric Association, 2020). This condition is most often discussed for military veterans, but it is widespread among different nationalities, occupations, ethnicities, and age groups, including children. Females are two to three times more likely to experience PTSD than their male counterparts, and it has been shown that PTSD has a significant impact on brain development (U.S. Department of Veterans Affairs, 2019).

PTSD has been described as a memory disorder that differentially affects memories recalled involuntarily, known as involuntary interruptions, and voluntarily, known as involuntary interruptions. Involuntary interruptions are unwanted and vivid memories of the trauma that occurred. These memories are highly emotional and can often be debilitating, which has led psychologists to call these interruptions indelible images that intrude everyday functions long after the trauma has occurred (Dahlgren, 2014). The fact that these traumatic events often occurred far in the past has no bearing on the severity of these involuntary interruptions.

Voluntary interruptions occur spontaneously through trauma narratives. These disruptions are not as emotionally charged and are often characterized as disorganized and fragmented. Memories cloudy and challenging to describe fall into this category (Dahlgren, 2014). For example, the first survivor who shared her story in Part One, Elizabeth, cannot recount every single detail of each of the multiple sexual assaults she suffered as a child. She has segments of memory of each assault, but these recollections are fragmented.

These two types of interruptions create an immediate and often debilitating paradox. One is voluntary and vivid, causing unwanted disruption to a person's day. The other is voluntary and vague, and in severe cases, presents itself as total amnesia. From a neuropsychological standpoint, memory is explicit and implicit (Rubin et al., 2008). Elizabeth can recall where she lived and the schools she attended with deliberate retrieval. These autobiographical facts are classified as explicit memories, whereas implicit memories are triggered by environmental conditions (Sidran Institute, 2019). Elizabeth's recollection of the sights, smells (i.e., her father's cologne), touches (i.e., invasion of her private parts), and sounds present during her sexual assault as a seven-year-old are examples of implicit memories.

Internal wounds might be tricky for others to identify readily, but characteristics of PTSD are easy to detect in those suffering from it. Noticeable signs of emotional distress such as flashbacks, debilitating feelings of shame and blame, heightened arousal, and extreme withdrawal or avoidance are not easy to disguise. This emotional distress often occurs at inopportune times (Dahlgren, 2014). In sexual assault and abuse situations, the body goes into shock to protect itself from horrific and overwhelming feelings brought on by the assault (Hopper, 2018). Many survivors go into auto-pilot when going about their daily lives. They may experience difficulties concentrating, sleeping, and simply not thinking about the traumatic experience for some time (University of Northern Colorado, 2020).

Life dramatically changes after the trauma whenever life-changing, traumatic, or stressful events occur for the victim. If PTSD is left unaddressed, the post-traumatic response will most likely be triggered later in life due to this stress's accumulating effects (Chessen et al., 2011).

PTSD occurs because a victim is stripped of ordinary coping skills and techniques, and treatment for PTSD includes developing healthy coping mechanisms required to function in everyday life. When left untreated, a person with PTSD will repeatedly become overwhelmed by minor stressors to the point of shutting down. Suppose healthy coping mechanisms are not developed to counter the symptoms of PTSD. In that case, this person will be more susceptible to unhealthy behaviors such as substance abuse, self-harm, and suicide (Center for Substance Abuse Treatment, 2014).

Recent work done by a Canadian psychologist and author Ann Wetmore has shown how a PTSD diagnosis funnels through four distinct categories, evidenced by the narratives above: intrusion, avoidance, negative thoughts or moods, and arousal. (Wetmore, 2019).

Intrusion is characterized as having intense flashbacks in which the victim revisits the traumatic event through either memory triggers or feeling triggers. Memory triggers cause the senses to be hyper-activated, whereas feeling triggers cause profound fear, sleeplessness, nervousness, and restlessness. Intrusion can be debilitating due to its ability to drive obsessive thinking about the event, causing the brain to operate on auto-pilot. Nightmares are also common with intrusion and cause the victim to relive the traumatic event in horrific, disturbing manners that are often worse than the actual traumatic event itself (Wetmore, 2019).

Avoidance is characterized by concerted efforts on the victim's part to forget the traumatic event altogether. Behavior is changed to avoid triggers caused by the trauma, and victims will often self-isolate to avoid talking about the trauma with others. A victim practicing avoidance will stop finding enjoyment in social events and gatherings and stop planning for their future (Wetmore, 2019).

Negative thoughts or moods and vicious negative self-talk in which the victim blames themselves for the trauma they suffered are pervasive. They experience hopelessness and will often feel as if they're permanently damaged. Numbness can occur due to negative self-talk, making it challenging to express love and affection toward others. It is common for one to become obsessed with these negative thoughts or moods and feel as if the world is doomed. Like avoidance, detachment from others can occur (Wetmore, 2019).

Arousal can be viewed as the opposite of avoidance as the victim is hyper or keyed-up and will exhibit a constant state of argumentativeness and irritability. Victims can be hyper-vigilant and always on the lookout for danger, which can cause them to be easily startled in extremes and become hypersensitive to loud, sudden noises. Fear of sleeping is expected with arousal, and the victim will often have persistent insomnia. Difficulties concentrating on simple tasks can occur, and the victim often exhibits unhealthy coping mechanisms such as self-harm and substance abuse (Wetmore, 2019; U.S. Department of Veterans Affairs, 2020).

In children who have experienced trauma, learning challenges can arise due to the effects of trauma on the brain. In Massachusetts, a dedicated team of child welfare advocates from the Massachusetts Advocates for Children partnered with students at Harvard Law School to create comprehensive training guides for educators called the Trauma and Learning Policy Initiative's (TLPI) to ensure that children exposed to adverse childhood experiences (ACEs) have the resources and support to excel academically, emotionally, and socially. The TLPI reviewed research around trauma's impact on child development and found that recent neurobiological, epigenetic, and psychological studies confirmed that traumatic experiences in early childhood could adversely affect focus, retention of information, executive functioning, and language development in children. Because these developmental skills are necessary for excelling academically and socially, children who have undergone trauma can struggle to perform at grade level, behave appropriately, and maintain relationships with their peers. When educators understand how trauma affects the brain, they are better positioned to provide the proper support and guidance to meet that child's needs (Trauma and Learning Policy Initiative, n.d.).

When interacting with children who have experienced trauma or abuse, it is essential to remember that developmental skills such as staying on task when given an assignment, self-regulating emotions and behaviors, and communicating properly might have been delayed because of the trauma. A traumatized child might struggle with self-esteem or experience tremendous anxiety around completing simple tasks (National Child Traumatic Stress Network, 2003; Trauma and Learning Policy Initiative, n.d.).

As discussed earlier, educators must respond in a trauma-informed manner to not further traumatize the child. When educators recognize trauma responses and implement trauma-informed techniques to support a child, they have a greater chance of succeeding (National Child Traumatic Stress Network, n.d.).

While PTSD can develop in children who have experienced trauma, other trauma-related disorders can occur, such as Acute Stress Disorder (ASD), Adjustment Disorder, Reactive Attachment Disorder (RAD), Disinhibited Social Engagement Disorder (DSED), or another trauma or stress-related disorder (Virginia Commission on Youth, 2017). If you are an educator or individual who works closely with children, please refer any child dealing with trauma to a licensed mental health professional for a proper diagnosis. Licensed mental health professionals can also properly facilitate a child's implementation of healthy coping techniques when dealing with stress or challenging situations (National Child Traumatic Stress Network, 2003). The following section will discuss practices that can be employed to manage trauma-related stress. When these interventions are put into place early on, children and adolescents will develop a well-rounded approach to help manage stress in a constructive manner that can be carried into adulthood.

SIX RESEARCH-BASED PRACTICES FOR RELIEVING TRAUMA-RELATED STRESS

When assisting young people exposed to trauma, the following have been noted as effective in mitigating the damaging effects of trauma-related stress (Harris, 2014).

1. Sleep

The CDC estimates that 70 million Americans are plagued with chronic sleep disorders. Sleep patterns are deeply affected when the night-time brain wrestles with the day's issues. As stressful thoughts develop, the stress hormone cortisol kicks into high gear, interrupting the condition of rest. Adverse effects can accumulate over time in the body, causing chronic diseases that adversely affect the quality of life. Dr. Burke-Harris notes that sleep helps recalibrate both the stress response and the immune system. Most adults need a consistent, uninterrupted seven- to nine-hour sleep cycle regularly to get the benefits of healthy sleep.

For individuals who have undergone trauma during childhood and adolescence, sleep is crucial to managing symptoms of PTSD. However, researchers specializing in sleep disorders have found that 90% of adults with PTSD have insomnia. Sleep-disordered breathing and erratic limb movements are also found in this population. People with PTSD also do not sleep as deeply as those who are healthy (Sleep Foundation, 2021). For example, Janet, a survivor who was raped 20 years ago and has complex PTSD, is awakened in the middle of the night by specific triggers: her child restlessly tossing in the middle of the night, a car coming to a screeching halt outside her apartment which makes her fearful someone is after her, and the air conditioner turning on prompting her to check all the doors and windows in search of possible intruders.

Arianna Huffington, the author of *The Sleep Revolution*, asks a universal question: "How much sleep is enough for the brain to function at full throttle?" (Huffington, 2016). After reviewing thousands of peer-reviewed articles from the American Academy of Sleep Medicine in a 2015 study, it was determined that a minimum of seven hours of sleep a night is essential for conditions of optimal health (American Academy of Sleep Medicine, 2015). Additionally, the National Sleep Foundation released the following information about optimal sleep cycles by age group. School-age children need 9-11 hours of sleep, teenagers need 8-10 hours, and adults need between 7-9 hours (Singh, 2021; Vyas, 2020).

For trauma survivors, it is crucial to be mindful of how trauma can impact their ability to attain quality sleep. When the mind is triggered by reminders of the trauma, symptoms such as racing heartbeat, breathing irregularities, grinding teeth or jaw clenching, excessive sweating, nightmares, and intrusive memories affect sleep quality. Some survivors experience only one of the symptoms, while others exhibit all of them. Sleep experts recommend that individuals practice these techniques to improve sleep quality: going to bed at a regular time nightly, winding down with brain relaxation exercises one hour before bed, avoiding stimulants such as alcohol, nicotine, cocoa, and caffeine before bed, exercising regularly (as intentional movement creates a better internal environment for sleep), using daylight efficiently to set one's biological clock to a predictable rhythm, avoiding daytime sleeping by napping for no longer than 20 to 30 minutes, eating early, journaling before bed, and only drinking water if awakened in the middle of the night (Sleep Foundation, 2021).

Be mindful of students who seem to doze off frequently in class, as this is one of the first indicators that they may not be getting adequate sleep. Sharing strategies to help combat sleep deprivation with students can be an essential step in the ongoing healing process.

2. Exercise

There is no shortage of excellent resources for regular exercise and good nutrition practices. Despite the plethora of information on the importance of regular exercise and good nutrition that ranges from simple to complex, one fact remains – the mind and body function better with a regular dose of exercise. Regular exercise burns up stress hormones and releases endorphins, our bodies' natural high-inducing chemicals. This, in turn, helps to stabilize our mood. Exercise releases something called brain-derived neurotrophic factor (BDNF), which is like MiracleGrow for brain cells as it allows the brain to make new connections and thrive more successfully. Incorporating mindfulness, breathing, and meditation into an exercise routine can also recharge the body by turning off one's thinking to allow the body to rest and digest. When we rest, it activates the parasympathetic nervous system to fight off adverse effects. Wendi Suzuki's TedTalk on the brain-changing benefits of exercise further notes the impact of exercise on brain health (Suzuki, 2017). Exercise is beneficial for all young people, but it might be especially vital for youth healing from trauma. Building movement breaks into classroom activities and exposing young people to a wide variety of options for physical activity and exercise, as well as teaching them about the multitude of benefits of exercise when it comes to mitigating stress, might be the motivating impetus to get young people, especially those healing from trauma, on a healthier path to recovery.

3. Nutrition

Because of the complex risk factors of youth who face trauma, there's a high likelihood that many children exposed to or healing from high levels of trauma don't have access to high-quality, nutrient-dense food regularly, let alone a sound knowledge base of the importance of nutrition in all brain and bodily functions, including mitigating trauma-related stress. Although many school nutrition programs have come a long way in recent years, there is still work to be done to provide young people with balanced, nutritious meals. Modeling healthy food choices and educating young people on the impact of healthy nutrition on overall wellness and healing is essential, as is advocating for schools to continue to provide healthier food options for students.

When it comes to education, an easy way to sabotage a solid nutrition program is to make it more complicated than it needs to be. Like exercise options, there are more dietary programs available today than ways to order coffee at Starbucks. More choices are not always better, so let's start with some simple basics. The "Choose My Plate" program developed through the U.S. Department of Agriculture (USDA) offers suggestions for starting fresh with an effective nutrition plan through graphics, videos, recipes, and much more. The resources provided by the U.S. Department of Agriculture (USDA) are user-friendly for both adults and children with age-appropriate videos to build knowledge about nutritional basics (U.S. Department of Agriculture, n.d.).

4. Mindfulness

One of the reasons mindfulness practices have become so popular is because they provide some of the best techniques for managing stress, depression, and anxiety. Mindfulness is the polar opposite of stress. In a state of distress, consuming, negative thoughts run rampant through our minds. During this state, breathing is shallow, tense, and a cramped perception is evident. Conversely, when we engage in mindful practices, we relax, our mind processes at a slower pace, and our breathing becomes evenly-paced, which can, in turn, positively affect how we process the world around us (University of Washington, 2017).

With the practice of mindfulness, we can hope to achieve what is called the "quiet mind," which produces a polar opposite response to the pedal-to-the-metal restless mind. Instead of preoccupation and avoidance, the quiet mind is present and has no other need than to be alive, responsive, peaceful, and accepting. Intuition, creativity, and inspiration are found in the quiet mind, and practicing this kind of tranquility counterbalances the restless mind's chaos, control, constant analysis, and judgment. The calm mind finds joy, acceptance, freedom, and the sheer privilege of being alive as its goals. This state of mind finds the act of regular gratitude a natural opioid. That's how powerful our inner mind functions. Feeling connected, accepted, free from debilitating thoughts or emotions, and released to love others with compassion and empathy are worthy goals in and of themselves (Minahan, 2019).

The production of cortisol, the stress hormone, through fear, worry, and anxiety negatively impacts physical and mental well-being. Conversely, through mindfulness training, we can create conditions of calm and tranquility that trigger the happy hormones to give us healing and improved health. Even taking 15 seconds of intentional time to develop thoughts of appreciation, positive self-talk, and gratitude statements can make all the difference in the world.

It's possible to use this notice-shift-rewire strategy to teach young people to reframe how they look at relationships in their lives. For example, we can teach young people to meditate on the positive relationships we want to have in the future and see them in our minds. Then, we can plot steps toward making these relationships a reality in our lives. Then, we can feel what we desire and act on these feelings. We can go further with a mindfulness mantra like "I am deserving of love and respect in my life" or "Each person I meet today will know I care about them because I will be present with them."

Intentional, well-practiced routines like the following five steps can be incredibly useful in getting to a more mindful state (Strosahl & Robinson, 2015). Step one is observing or noticing things happening inside you (physical sensations, thoughts, feelings, memories) and outside you (sights, sounds, colors, faces, activities, others' reactions, etc.). Step two involves describing the sensations you are experiencing using words that convey your experiences. Strosahl and Robinson call this "being a witness," with the motive to tell the truth and nothing but the truth. Step three challenges you to detach from the traumatic experience holding you back. Detaching means that we are not anchored down by evaluation, critique, blame, shame, or analysis and instead are letting go of thoughts, memories, or events that have been painful in the past. With detachment comes the practice of remembering painful experiences but then learning how to move past them. Step four is a radical step as it calls you to love yourself. On the journey toward achieving a "quiet mind," loving yourself is the key to tranquility and peace. Finally, step five calls us to "act intentionally." This phase includes behaving in a way that reflects your values and beliefs while accepting that this step takes time and patience to master. We are all prone to impulsive behaviors that do not represent the attitude of the heart, so we can model and teach students how to give themselves grace and practice self-compassion when working toward this level of mindfulness.

5. Other Mindfulness Practices.

Mindfulness does not always have to be meditation. It can encompass activities that allow one to be present and centered. Below are some unconventional mindfulness practices to help students explore mindfulness in new and different ways.

Novelty. Breaking old habits can be challenging, but our mind seeks new and different experiences created through novelty. For example, suppose you see a student stuck in the habit of doing things the same way every day. In that case, you can help them stimulate their brain by encouraging them to try a new way of solving a problem or participate in a new activity at recess. The goal is to train the brain to enjoy new experiences and live in the moment.

The Importance of Play. Play is about intentionally seeking enjoyment, not out of competition, but simply out of joy. This can be difficult for some experiencing depression and deep trauma, but it is entirely possible through practice. Play is vital for well-being. The fact remains that students' school days are often so jammed with content that often exercise, recess or creative play get chopped from the pressure-cooked schedule. This adversely affects a child's development, and educators must emphasize the benefits of play to a child's emotional, psychological, and physical well-being and work to protect these times of constructive play within the school day. Even teenagers need regular opportunities to engage in play-based activities like games, which can be directly integrated into content-based learning opportunities.

Gratitude. Our young people are growing up in a society that lives, eats, and breathes in excess, which creates an "I am not enough" attitude. When we are helping young people shift from survival mode to spaces where they can thrive, gratitude practices can be a valuable tool to teach young people to employ. Something as simple as having them create a list of what makes them "enough" is a positive gratitude practice. Below are examples of student-created "I Am/I Have" statements that came about as a result of this positive practice activity:

• I am loved, and I am finding ways to be successful in small steps.

- I have everything I need right now to be happy. I will rest in it.
- I am finding new ways to be creative and alive by reading positive books, going to the library, walking in a new area of town, etc.
- I am living in a safe place where I can grow and learn.
- I am contributing to making my relationships fun, happy, and healthy.
- I am building a bank of great memories daily in the classroom.
- I am creating ways to appreciate those around me by performing acts of kindness that take me away from my present condition of grief (depression, anxiety, stress, worry, anger, etc.)
- I am invested in being the person people want to be around.

You could take this single activity a step further by having each student create a Positivity Journal written and dated all year long to chronicle their thought life.

6. Healthy Relationships

It is common for survivors of traumatic events such as sexual exploitation to experience difficulties maintaining healthy relationships. Healthy bonding is built upon trust, compromise, mutual respect, freedom to express opinions through open communication, and understanding. In sexual exploitation, there is a polar opposite: lack of communication, little or no trust, issues surrounding control, lack of healthy boundaries, possessiveness, and a lack of independence. It is crucial to support young people in working with a licensed mental health professional when establishing healthy relationships and boundaries with individuals (Brickel, 2021). A key component of establishing these healthy, supportive relationships is forgiveness, which can be done under the guidance of a licensed therapist to help youth process the anger, hurt, and betrayal necessary to forgive.

Forgiveness does not necessarily lead to reconciliation. When it comes to most survivors of sexual exploitation and violent crimes, the perpetrators will need to be removed from their lives altogether. However, many of the featured survivors in this book stated that they decided to forgive their perpetrators not to accommodate or excuse the abusers but heal for their well-being. They did remove the perpetrators from their lives, but forgiveness released the survivors from the poisonous rage that was trapped inside and destroying their mental and physical health. While on the journey of forgiveness, understand that it is ultimately a choice that does not happen overnight. For most survivors, it may take years to decide to take even the first step toward forgiveness. And even after the conscious decision is made, one must do the work to process the trauma and rewrite negative mental narratives to forgive.

Aside from forgiveness, another crucial component for re-establishing healthy relationships is learning appropriate communication skills and ways to express emotions. As mentioned earlier, it is essential that any survivor who has been traumatized work with a therapist or other licensed mental health professional when learning these skills. Journaling is an excellent way to take inventory of one's thoughts and feelings and help center oneself when dealing with stressful events. A therapist might request a patient write a letter to a person who has hurt them and instruct the patient to wait for some time before sending it or destroying it. As survivors learn how to communicate effectively, these outlets are great ways to release stress and anxiety and process frustration that comes from doing this work.

Regardless of your specific role in supporting children and adolescents who have been traumatized, having the skills and knowledge to help them prioritize their mental health and well-being will keep them on their paths to living healthy, balanced lives. As this chapter discussed, you can help students implement many self-care strategies and practices in their daily life, thus developing greater agency as they continue to deal with the plethora of circumstances that may be beyond their control. Do not be discouraged if students reject a specific strategy or practice. Remember that everyone responds differently to particular techniques and methods, and they might have to try several approaches before finding the one that works for them. Many survivors have found these practices to be of great value on their healing journey to living healthy, whole, and prosperous lives. Being aware of and practicing these strategies in our own lives can also help us support the healing of survivors as we engage with them.

CONCLUSION

My calling as an educator has allowed me to work in educational settings beyond the traditional classroom. One such setting was a community youth center designed to provide a healthy place for adolescents and their families to connect through various fun, age-appropriate activities. As the center's director, I learned that not all of the adults I encountered, the eager individuals who wanted to volunteer as chaperones, mentors, foster parents, or scout leaders, had pure intentions. Not all children were fortunate enough to come from homes of attentive and involved parents. I had met children who had been bullied and subjected to physical and mental abuse and sexual exploitation. These children became the purpose behind our work at the Youth Center, and I became a child welfare advocate without knowing what that entailed. As each predator was revealed, my team swiftly became an army of advocates, informing law enforcement and child protective services of abuse so that they could provide the proper safeguards we could not offer. We were grateful that the courts removed these predators from the community so that they could not hurt another child; however, many children who had also experienced abuse in the home were unfortunately placed back into the care of abusive parents due to the court's intentions of keeping families together. Many abusive parents and guardians received light sentences such as eight weeks of parenting classes and individual therapy. They continued the pattern of abuse once they completed the courses and mandated therapy.

As I transitioned into raising my family, I left my position as the youth center director, carrying the experiences of these vulnerable children with me as I ventured back into the classroom as a middle school teacher years later.

However, I knew, at some point, I would circle back to those experiences, accompanied by my recent experiences working "with" and "for" children and adults, to write the stories that were still in my heart. In every role I have served in, the children I encountered have remained with me, whether in my role as a teacher, coach, mentor, or district curriculum specialist. After 27 years in the classroom and five years in a district office, my love for education took me throughout the U.S. and abroad in service to thousands of dedicated educators as an educational consultant. Those 15 years were among the most exciting and productive years of my life. However, the time eventually came to leave the grueling travel and training schedule and begin enjoying my role as a fully engaged grandmother to my 17 amazing grandchildren. They reminded me that my work was not finished, that I had to honor the children who impacted my life all those years ago. With this renewed dedication to amplifying the stories of sexual exploitation and childhood trauma survivors, I thoroughly reviewed case studies around abuse and trauma, studied research on the brain, PTSD, OCD, and subsequent mental health issues resulting from trauma, and worked to understand the role generational dysfunction contributes to our narratives. The culmination of all these experiences led to a divine meeting with Christy as we began framing this project. Christy's passion for eradicating child sex trafficking and exploitation through education, awareness, restoration projects, and justice initiatives worked in tandem with my heart and expertise, which led to the collaborative effort that you're now holding in your hands.

Adversity introduces each human to themselves. Though I did not experience sexual exploitation, my life has been significantly influenced by the traumatic remnants of alcoholism and witnessing domestic disputes in my home as a child. And in recent years, deep trauma revisited our family, in the form of the deaths of 11 significant loved ones. The departures occurred within a very short period, making it nearly impossible to grieve the life before another was gone. Some deaths were expected, due to old age and ill health, while other scenarios shortened the lives of our very young, surrounded by unexpected, painful circumstances. Because of these experiences, I intimately understand loss, penetrating-to-the-bone pain, PTSD, sleeplessness, depression, flashbacks, and the like. The unexpected death of my 56-year old husband left me nearly catatonic. And I have been very deliberate in choosing a path that has led to a life of resilience, joy, contentment, and wholeness. But it has been an enormous journey and worth every ounce of effort!

We don't have to have it all together. We are all in progress. However, open, honest dialogue allows us to heal, reconcile, and repurpose. I believe our own fractured, personal stories have the potential of making us significantly stronger and more beautiful than our original selves, similar to the beautiful, restorative Japanese art of Kintsugi. Essentially, each of our stories becomes a conduit of hope and healing when shared. The sincere goal of all the experts and survivors who contributed to this work is that these authentic stories may spur something special in your heart to become a freedom fighter alongside us.

With issues as dire as the sexual exploitation and trafficking of children, it is crucial to reach out to individuals from all walks of life who are committed to the welfare of children. As more information becomes available about childhood trauma, the mental and emotional health challenges caused by sexual exploitation and human trafficking, and the effectiveness of community-based initiatives in combating these crimes, everyone in our communities must lend a helping hand in tackling the epidemic of sexual exploitation and human trafficking. This is not a problem that can be solved individually. It requires the expertise and collaboration of every caring adult in our school, church, community, and home.

As every story you have read demonstrates, no one chooses a life of abuse and neglect. We must keep this fact in our hearts and minds as we all become first responders in our communities. We must always lead with compassion and humility, building bridges instead of walls, to include all children born into diverse family structures and with multiple belief systems. In closing, I offer you one of Mother Teresa's compelling quotes appropriate for both first responders and survivors when circumstances become challenging: "Not all of us can do great things. But we can do small things with great love." I have learned personally that there is no such thing as an insignificant act when it comes to the welfare of our children. All I need to do is listen and attend. In essence, love is the universal language that connects one to another, and it comes without expecting a reward. Giving is living. Helping one helps us all.

GRATITUDE

LAURIE

Quiet reflection is a profound teacher. This book has been a valuable journey of attempting to understand the mind and actions of beautiful people who have endured situations that no child or adult should ever have to endure. We all process differently. We hear conversations differently. Our reactions and perceptions are seen through different filters. Through countless hours of researching, interviewing, observing, listening, and reflecting, I will never have the capacity to fully understand what it is like to live in the dark places of sexual exploitation as these survivors have. I write in the context of an educator, a child advocate, and a lifelong "first responder." With that voice, I deeply respect, protect, and honor the courage of each survivor who spoke truth into this text. I feel the essence of Gibran's words express my sentiments the best. "Let us be so connected to one another that when one weeps, the other tastes salt." We are all in need of grace, and it meets us each day exactly where we are; flaws and imperfections accepted. Grace means there is no need to airbrush the imperfections in our life to pretend to be someone we are not. We are all in progress and made new every morning.

The landscape from which I write is one of faith and belief that even though we travel through life differently, we all are entitled to equal access to be happy and whole. That journey will never be easy or linear. Involvement in the lives of others is very complex and comes without a formula. For those reasons, it is so much easier to disengage and shy away from topics such as sexual exploitation and human trafficking, much less write a book about the horrific experiences so many have faced alone. The scars from traumatic experiences force most victims to stuff the shame rather than deal with it. But to avoid the topic is to turn our backs on those who need our help and support. Choosing involvement in matters such as this are messy... confusing... conflicting, and frustrating! At the same time, it is invigorating, challenging, motivating, and life-changing! While writing this book, there has been a taste of those elements, and tremendous growth and understanding have resulted.

These reflections have certainly held in the process of collaborating with my friend and colleague, Christy Ivie, president and founder of Christy's Cause. Christy, your contributions as a trauma-informed leader made the content of this manuscript more authentic because it represents the true voice of survivors. Thank you for choosing the "just right" front-row experts to partner with us as they spoke their expertise into a balanced, survivor-centered finished product. Christy's Cause has been successful because of your thoughtful planning, selective alignment to quality projects, and choice of well-informed people who have developed into lifelong relationships – core values we both highly revere.

Over the past four years, I have keenly observed how you work with heart and inner guidance. Compassion and genuine love are apparent in what you do. You have intimately helped me understand how survivors carry the shame of sexual exploitation even decades after the fact, and due to personal shame, their stories are kept secret. We have experienced firsthand the warfare involved in sharing stories of tough, raw content such as this. But I am confident that by honoring survivors and sharing their bravery with our readers, we have held out for the greater good, and lives will be profoundly influenced by our sincere efforts to inform, support, and respond.

Dearest Elizabeth, you are a strong, unbelievable woman! Thank you for having the courage to share your harrowing story so others may break free from their incidents of trauma. You are courageous for fighting the darkness of victimhood and cautiously stepping into the light as a surviving, thriving, "steel magnolia." Thank you for trusting me with your story. As you took me through the brutal realities of your childhood, I applaud you for never giving up. It is my greatest hope that by mustering the courage to speak on your behalf, your message of hope will open the floodgates for millions of others who believe they don't have the strength to stand up for themselves. I know how costly it was for you to share vignettes that had never been shared with even the closest people in your life. I know intimately that your purest goal was to stand beside those who have felt shamed and silenced. Hope and resilience spring from your bravery. You risked being exposed and vulnerable on behalf of others, a very unselfish goal. I will always hold your story with integrity and advocacy. You are a respected woman for your valiant efforts to be proactive and authentic.

My sincere gratitude to each brave survivor who shared so willingly with the same purpose as Christy and Elizabeth. Though you have all come from different locations and diverse demographics, be encouraged that armies of people applaud your bravery as you have shared your vulnerabilities so others will be made aware. You deserve to step into the future vital and whole by addressing first the wounds of the past so that a bright future can emerge. Bravo, my friends! You are on the road to reclaiming the future because you are willing to rise and seek help.

To educators past and present, thank you for your tireless efforts as first responders for your students. Keep in mind that our role is never to attempt to replace a licensed therapist, counselor, or law enforcement. Our greater calling is to teach and reach! Planning for and executing robust academic instruction daily is task enough as an educator, but now layer on the monumental task of attending to each student's complex emotional and physical needs. This cannot be done effectively in a silo. That's where the efficacy of TEAM takes support to a higher level. (administration, teachers, counselors, law enforcement, parents, social services, etc.). Silo mentality proves unsuccessful and very personally and professionally draining. Your commitment to the profession is admired and respected, despite the obstacles and mandates of public and private education. Your strong advocacy and influence are vital in impacting the lives of 21st-century children.

As I became serious about committing the time it takes to accurately write the stories, gather the research, and provide supportive resources and tools with awareness and understanding for the reader, the "just right" publisher needed to be selected. My trusted friend and gentle giant, Douglas Rife, connected me to Full Circle Press. What a great match this has been! Thank you to Sibyl Perez, Jared Dixon, and especially Dr. Marina Gillmore for your diligence and professionalism in producing a quality finished product. Marina, your patience and stability through rewrites and all the intricacies of publishing have proven to be exceptional. I have been refreshed and enriched by your thoughtful, mature, and thorough mind and your commitment to advocacy for the under-represented, a hallmark of your work at Full Circle Press. Laura, you listened to the inner workings behind the text and created a cover that brought Christy and me to tears when you first presented it to us! Thank you for articulating precisely the message we wanted through your artful graphics and the accompanying manuscript layout. The entire Full Circle Press team has exhibited impeccable integrity – one of our highest values.

I extend my deepest respect and gratitude to my family, friends, and trusted colleagues who have championed efforts to fight sexual exploitation and abuse of any kind that preys upon the vulnerabilities of innocent children. May we remain united as we continue to stand in the gap for those whose voices have been silenced or snuffed out.

I am beyond grateful to my dear husband, Hank, who has literally seen me glued to this endeavor for the past four years. A more faithful friend and confidant I could not ask for, my love. Through countless hours of required study, missed meals, and the need for quiet focus, you have been a solid, stable cheerleader through it all. To our beloved adult children and their spouses, Aaron (Tiffany), Heather (Justin), Carson (Michelle), Maggie (Jeremy), and

Drew (Cassie), oh how it brings joy to my heart to see you nurture and instruct your tribe. Let service to others continue to be your trademark. I am inspired beyond words by your leadership, both private and public, as co-constructors of a brighter future. Thank you for having the guts to ACT, THRIVE, and BE. I love you all so much!

To our 17 beautiful grandchildren, I pray your lives will be like lighthouses, having the ability to identify and maneuver through the complexities of our current, confusing world. Hold on to the "light" to bring you safe harbor and security. You are so deeply loved, Avi, Alia, Halle, Liam, Levi, Elijah, Olivia, Isaac, Josie, Eli, Nate, Libby, J.D, Karson, Karlie, Benji, and Henry. (Whew, I made it in one breath!)

To each reader engaged in the stories of this book, Christy and I give our sincere thanks for allowing us the opportunity to hopefully cause a bit of a "stir" in your soul, calling you to act on behalf of those whose solitary cries fall on deaf ears. Though we have specifically targeted educators in the writing of this book, we are confident that if you are reading this as a parent, neighbor, community member, or critical friend, you find your role as a treasured and vital "first responder." As a fellow protector of the planet, wherever your eyes land on the pages of this book, we honor and respect your individual beliefs and are privileged to share these scenarios in a way that will hopefully heighten your senses as you are invited to reflect and respond. Through continuing conversations, we all see with a more refined and informed lens, which drives our actions.

It only takes observation and heart to truly SEE the misery so many carry alone. Collectively, let's pick up a cup of flavored coffee and fresh cookies and BE the audience "for" and "with" one who sits across the table and says, "Do YOU care to know me?" Thank you, dear ones. Together...Onward and Upward!

CHRISTY

After several years and what seemed like a thousand rewrites and edits, it's hard to believe we hold *One Story, Many Voices* in our hands. There is no way to write about such in-depth topics as child sex trafficking and sexual exploitation without a team of brilliant people investing countless hours and tons of brainpower. I still remember meeting over breakfast as Laurie and I started discussing the possibilities of this book. We shared a mutual desire to give survivors an anonymous platform where their voices could be heard in a safe arena while incorporating research and resources for educators to better understand the epidemic of sexual exploitation our children face. Her legacy of advocating for abused children impressed me. I could see her desire to collaborate to develop a helpful resource for educators working with children who have their own survival stories. And so, we began the journey.

Thank you, Laurie, for your dedication as an advocate for children. The investment of your time and resources has been invaluable in bringing this project to fruition. Although you have worked with children who have survived sexual abuse over the years, you have taken on the challenge to better understand the trauma that affects many survivors. Your passion for equipping educators with resources to help them on their journey of becoming trauma-informed has impressed me. I am forever grateful to you for giving voiceless survivors a safe platform to speak. Thank you for the investment you made in writing *One Story, Many Voices.*

To all the survivors who courageously shared their stories, I am in awe of your bravery. I know how triggering seeing your story in print can be. I know the wave of emotion you battled to get to this point. Your sacrifice has laid a foundation for many to find freedom. *One Story, Many Voices* would not be what it is without you. Thank you. Thank you for sharing your truth with grace and dignity. I am honored to partner with each one of you.

Thank you to all the professionals who work tirelessly in combating child sex trafficking and exploitation who invested their time and expertise as contributors for *One Story, Many Voices.* Your feedback guided our journey. Laurie and I are forever grateful for the investment you made in this project. We know we share the same dream – to be part of a world where children are safe and able to thrive. Thank you for your advocacy. Thank you for all you do for children behind the scenes, where most never know.

I have been so impressed with the team at Full Circle Press. This project has been a significant undertaking requiring countless hours and a tremendous heart of advocacy. Dr. Gillmore, you have been a fearless leader that has calmed my anxious heart many times. Thank you for your dedication. Thank you for going the extra mile when you didn't need to. Your character has shone through, and I am honored to have worked with you and your team. *One Story, Many Voices* most definitely would not have come to fruition without you!

A huge thank you to the board and advisors who serve Christy's Cause! Your leadership, friendship, and wisdom guided my path. I am honored to have such a dedicated team of advocates working alongside me whom I call friends. Your hearts beat for children! Each one of you brought valuable insight to this project, for which I am forever grateful. Thank you for the investment you continually make.

I'm so blessed to have an inner circle of diverse and amazing friends who gave me safe spaces to process aspects of this book. Your honest feedback gave me perspective from different viewpoints, which was much needed. Your voices represent professionals working with survivors making the wisdom you shared invaluable. Thank you for your words of encouragement when I needed them the most, often out of the blue but timely. I am more grateful than you will ever know.

A special thank you to my daughter, who also serves on the board. You are such a freedom fighter! You give me the courage to be braver. You are always in my corner. You always have the best advice. How did I manage to be selected to be your mom? You are my best friend and confidant. To say I love you to the moon and back is not enough. Maybe I love you thiiiiiiiiiiiiiiiiiiis much? Still not enough. My Songbird, my baby girl, my best friend. I love you!

To my firstborn, my son – the day you were born, you brought so much healing to my heart. Having the opportunity to be your mom healed places in my broken spirit others couldn't seem to touch. I smile every time I hug you now, as you tower over me, and I think about days long ago when your little hand stayed in mine wherever we went. You've become a dad now and have a little hand in yours. That makes my heart very, very happy. I love you so very much!

I am incredibly blessed to have two sets of parents that have been given to me as a gift from the Lord – Bill & Judy Ivie and Tom & Jan Lane. I didn't have the opportunity to know loving, safe, nurturing parents in my childhood. Then miraculously, God brought you to me. You have shown me what it is like to love unconditionally, you have modeled healthy loving marriages, you have given me the best advice, and prayed for me through the darkest nights. This book would not be without you. You gave me the courage to speak simply by being in my life. I am forever indebted to the four of you.

To my husband, my safe place, my rock. How would I exist without you? How would I untangle myself without your constant assistance? I have been forever changed by your love. You steady me, calm me, and give me the courage to continue moving forward. You push me never to accept the status quo. Thank you for all your comforting words of encouragement and, most importantly, the moments you just listened and gave me space to process (and untangle myself). I love you with my whole heart.

ABOUT THE AUTHORS

Laurie Sammons is a passionate educator who invested 45 years as an elementary teacher, middle school English teacher, district curriculum specialist, youth center director, gymnastic coach, reading specialist, and adjunct college professor. For the last 15 years of her career (2004-2019), she was a national consultant for Solution Tree, a premier professional development company, delivering site-based training to administrators and teacher teams across the United States and numerous foreign countries. The primary focus of her work has included strategic planning, collaborative leadership, and best practice instructional strategies to engage students across academic disciplines, age groups, and varied cognitive abilities. In 2006, she was selected as a delegate in the Fulbright Teacher Ambassador program to study educational reform in Japan. In addition to writing several educational publications, she is co-author of the book *Handbook for Unstoppable Learning* (2018) and a contributing author of a book written by gerontologist Lori Campbell, *Awaken Your Age Potential: Exploring Chosen Paths of Thrivers* (2012). Through Laurie's intimate work with youth and families in communities, schools, and numerous mission trips to developing countries, she and her family have been keenly awakened to the many acts of sexual exploitation, bullying, suicide, and other matters of domestic violence, which led to the writing of this book. Laurie and her husband split their time between Southwest Florida and the beautiful hills of West Virginia and love nothing more than traveling to visit their five children and 17 grandchildren who live throughout the world.

Christy Ivie founded Christy's Cause in 2015 and leads the organization, bringing over 14 years of experience in strategy development and operations management in both profit and nonprofit sectors. Her experience has given her expertise in strategic planning, project management, construction management, business coaching, business startup, and business turnaround. "I've always known I would use my childhood story to reach out and help children who are at risk of sexual exploitation," Christy said. "I am excited to be a part of a unique and growing nonprofit organization that brings hope to an otherwise desperate and dark situation." Christy is passionate about life and exudes hope and positivity. "Freedom Fighter" is her life's motto which she lives out through the vision of Christy's Cause. You can learn more about her work at www.christyscause.com.

ABOUT THE CONTRIBUTORS

Special thanks to the following professionals who contributed their time, expertise, and passion on behalf of this book's mission to promote education, awareness, and prevention in helping to eradicate sexual exploitation and assault for men and women today and in the generations to come.

Christa Lynn is a licensed therapist in Florida, a certified clinical trauma professional, RYT 200 yoga instructor, and a second-generation survivor of sex trafficking. She is the founder of Into the Jordan, an organization providing direct services to adult trafficking survivors in SW Florida. Christa previously was the executive director of anti-trafficking at One More Child, which provides wrap-around services to sex-trafficked persons, a residential home for trafficked teens, and HT and trauma training. Christa is currently founding Salt Water Therapist, a new trauma therapy program for survivors centered around her love for the outdoors. Christa is a dedicated and compassionate woman who shares her experience as a trafficking survivor, her clinical expertise, and years of growth to continuously improve the services available to those being sold and exploited by others. You can follow Christa on her social media channels @Christalynnfmb or email her at saltwatertherapist@gmail.com.

Corporal Alan Wilkett has held an impeccable law enforcement career in the Pasco Sherriff's office for twenty-seven years relating to major crimes, narcotics, and child abuse. His proven record for leadership as a chief deputy, captain, commander, and director of public safety is stellar. His relentless passion for justice has been exhibited tirelessly in his pursuit of ending human trafficking in all of its deplorable forms. His work to eradicate human trafficking led to being recognized by Florida's Attorney General, Pam Bondi, as Human Trafficking Law Enforcement Official of the Year. The Florida Crime Prevention Association honored Corporal Wilkett with its Lifetime Achievement Award in October of 2019. He recently co-founded the Human Trafficking Foundation to enlarge further the scope of actions to wipe out this global epidemic of modern-day slavery.

Jennifer Wolff brings over 20 years as a Registered Nurse to include nursing education, public health education, administration, school nursing, and her passion in her current position as an emergency room/trauma nurse. In her ER nursing role working with victims, she spearheads a program, WeCare Nurses, developed by nurses, for nurses, to identify and treat victims of Human Trafficking while giving them tools they need to break free from their captors. Jenny and her family live in Southwest Florida.

We have been blessed to share curriculum conversations around sexual exploitation and human trafficking, especially during the past two academic years during COVID, with colleague **Laura Perry**, a Florida educator who planted the seed for the book title. Her wisdom, altruistic insight, and shared passion for building global awareness of sexual exploitation and creating a safer world for children of the 21st century have been a gift. Laura and her husband are residents of Naples, Florida.

Thanks to **Val Gill**, a client-focused life coach and therapist, for dialogue around mindful practices and effective tools and strategies for survivors dealing with PTSD, OCD, and various mental conditions associated with trauma. Val founded and leads Mindful Presence Therapy, which can be found online at www.mindfulpresencetherapy.com. Val resides in Fort Myers, Florida.

ABOUT FULL CIRCLE PRESS

Full Circle Press is a socially conscious, purpose-driven hybrid publishing house with a deep commitment to contributing to the greater good through helping to write, edit, publish, and market books that matter. We believe in changing the world one story at a time, and we envision a world where quality books and literacy resources are available to all. We are educators at heart and are passionate about teaching what we know, sharing resources when and where we can, and empowering others to do and be better. Visit www. fullcirclepress.org to learn more about our products, programs, and services.

RESOURCES

If you are an adult and have been struggling with unresolved childhood trauma, contact SAMHSA at 1-800-662-HELP or visit their website www.samhsa.gov/find-help/national-helpline.

Visit www.childwelfare.gov/organizations to locate your state child abuse reporting numbers.

For additional support related to suspected human trafficking, contact the National Human Trafficking Hotline at 1-888-373-7888 or visit their website www.humantraffickinghotline.org.

Contact the National Center for Missing and Exploited Children for additional support related to missing children or child sexual exploitation. Contact the National Center for Missing and Exploited Children at 1-800-843-5678 or visit their websitewww.missingkids.org.

Please visit our website at www.onestorymanyvoices.com for more information on workshop training and additional support services available in collaboration with this book, as well as free resources for educators, families, and survivors.

REFERENCES

Abel, G., Harlow, N. (2001). *The stop child molestation book: What ordinary people can do in their everyday lives to save 3 million children.* Xlibris.

Aces Too High. (n.d.). *What ACEs/PCEs do you have?* Retrieved May 24, 2021 from, https://acestoohigh.com/got-your-ace-score/

Ahlmeyer, S., Heil, P., McKee, B., & English, K. (2000). The impact of polygraphy on admissions of victims and offenses in adult sexual offenders. *Sexual Abuse: A Journal of Research and Treatment, 12*(2), 123-138.

Amaro, Marie. (n.d.). *How to get a student to own their behavior.* The Highly Effective Teacher. Retrieved July 1, 2021 from, https://thehighlyeffectiveteacher.com/how-to-get-a-student-to-own-their behaviour/

American Academy of Sleep Medicine, (2015, June 1). *Seven or more hours of sleep per night: A healthy necessity for adults* [Press Release]. https://aasm.org seven-or-more-hours-of-sleep-per-night-a-health-necessity-for-adults/

American Psychiatric Association. (2020). *What is posttraumatic stress disorder?* https://www.psychiatry.org/patients-families/ptsd/what-is-ptsd

American Association of Neurological Surgeons. (2021). *Anatomy of the brain.* https://www.aans.org/en/Patients/Neurosurgical-Conditions-and-Treatments/Anatomy-of-the-Brain

American Psychological Association. (2017, July). *What is cognitive behavioral therapy?* https://www.apa.org/ptsd-guideline/patients-and-families/cognitive-behavioral

Baron, R. A., Byrne, D., Branscombe, N. R. (2006). *Social psychology* (11th ed). Pearson.

Bethell, C., Jones, J., Gombojav, N., Linkenbach, J., Sege, R. (2019). Positive childhood experiences and adult mental and relational health in a statewide sample: associations across adverse childhood experiences levels. *JAMA Pediatrics, 173*(11), e193007-e193007. doi:10.1001 jamapediatrics.2019.3007

Beyond Blue. (n.d.). *Strategies to support anxious children.* Retrieved July 1, 2021 from, https://healthyfamilies.beyondblue.org.au/age-6-12/mental-health-conditions-in-childrenanxiety/strategies-to-support-anxious-children

Bitsko, R. H., Holbrook, J. R., Ghandour, R. M., Blumberg, S. J., Visser, S. N., Perou, R., & Walkup, J. T. (2018). Epidemiology and impact of health care provider diagnosed anxiety and depression among US children. *Journal of Developmental and Behavioral Pediatrics* 39(5), 395-403. doi: 10.1097/DBP.0000000000000571

Brennan, D. (2020, November 20). *Signs of a sexual predator.* WebMD. https://www.webmd.com/sex-relationships/signs-sexual-predator

Brickel, R. (2021). *Having healthy sex and relationships after sexual abuse.* PsychAlive. https://www.psychalive.org/having-healthy-sex-and-relationships-after-sexual-abuse/

Casey Family Programs. (2017, December 29). *How does turnover affect outcomes and what can be done to address retention?* [Information Packet]. https://www.casey.org/turnover-costs-and-retention-strategies/

Centers for Disease Control and Prevention. (n.d.). *Preventing child sexual abuse.* Retrieved November 12, 2021 from, https://www.cdc.govviolenceprevention/childsexualabuse/fastfact.html

Center for Disease Control and Prevention. (2019, September 5). *Adverse childhood experiences (ACEs).* https://www.cdc.gov/vitalsigns/aces/index.html

Centers for Disease Control and Prevention. (2021, April 6). *About the CDC-Kaiser ACE study.* https://www.cdc.gov/violenceprevention/aces/about.html?CDC_AA_refVal https%3A%2F%2Fwww.cdc.gov%2Fviolenceprevention%2Facestudy%2Fabout.html

Center for Disease Control and Prevention. (2021, April 19). *Sexual violence is preventable.* https://www.cdc.gov/injury/features/sexual-violence/index.html

Center for Disease Control and Prevention. (2021, April 28). *Health and economic costs of chronic diseases.* https://www.cdc.gov/chronicdisease/about/costs/index.htm#ref1

Center for Substance Abuse Treatment. (2014). Trauma-informed care in behavioral health services. https://www.ncbi.nlm.nih.gov/books/NBK207191/

Center on the Developing Child. (2015). *In Brief: The science of resilience.* https://developingchild.harvard.edu/resources/inbrief-the-science-of-resilience/

Chessen, C. E., Comtois, K. A., & Landes, S. J. (2011). Untreated posttraumatic stress among persons with severe mental illness despite marked trauma and symptomatology. *Psychiatric Services, 62*(10), 1201-1206.

Chibnall, S., Dutch, N. M., Jones-Harden, B., Brown, A., Gourdine, R., Smith, J., Boone, A., Snyder, S. (2003, December). *Children of color in the child welfare system: Perspectives from the child welfare community.* Child Welfare Information Gateway. https://www.childwelfare.gov/pubs/otherpubs/children/implications/

Child Abuse Watch. (n.d.). *The three types of sexual predators.* Abuse Watch. Retrieved May 27, 2021 from, https://www.abusewatch.net/pred_sex.php

Child Liberation Foundation. (2020). *Child trafficking statistics.* May 27, 2021 from, https://liberatechildren.org/child-trafficking-statistics

Child Welfare Information Gateway. (2017). *Human trafficking and child welfare: A guide for caseworkers.* U.S. Department of Health and Human Services, https://www.childwelfare.gov/pubs/trafficking-caseworkers/

Child Welfare Information Gateway. (2019). *What is child abuse and neglect? Recognizing the signs and symptoms.* U.S. Department of Health and Human Services. https://www.childwelfare.gov/pubs/factsheets/whatiscan/

Child Welfare Information Gateway. (2020, October). *How the child welfare system works* [Factsheet]. U.S. Department of Health and Human Services. https://www.childwelfare.gov/pubPDFs/cpswork.pdf

Child Welfare League of America. (2020). *The nation's children 2020.* https://www.cwla.org/wp-content/uploads/2020/03/National-2020.pdf

Children's Defense Fund. (2021). *The state of America's children 2021.* https://www.childrensdefense.org/state-of-americas-children/soac-2021-child-welfare/

Clawson, H. J., Dutch, N., Solomon, A., & Grace, L. G. (2009). *Human trafficking into and within the United States: A review of the literature.* Office of the Assistant Secretary for Planning and Evaluation, U.S. Department of Human and Health Services. https://aspe.hhs.gov/report/human-trafficking-and-within-united-states-review-literature

Complex Trauma Treatment Network. (n.d). *Sparks.* Retrieved May 28, 2021 from, https://www.cttntraumatraining.org/sparcs.html

Council of Europe Convention. (2012, October). *Protection of children against sexual exploitation and sexual abuse.* Article 18. Retrieved November 8, 2021 from https://rm.coe.int/protection-of-children-against-sexual-exploitation-and-sexual-abuse/1680794e97

Cordua, J. (2019, April) *How we can eliminate child sexual abuse material from the internet* [Video File]. Retrieved May 24, 2021 from, https://www.ted.com/talks/julie_cordua_how_we_can_eliminate_child_sexual_abuse_material from_the_internet?language- en

Dahlgren, K. (2014, November 18). *Hooked on a feeling: intrusive and ruminative symptoms in PTSD.* Emotions, Brain, & Behavior Laboratory. https://sites.tufts.edu/emotiononthebrain/2014/11/18/hooked-on-a-feeling-intrusive and-ruminative-symptoms-in-ptsd/

Desautels, Lori. (2017, April 26). *Reaching students with emotional disturbances. Edutopia.* https://www.edutopia.org/article/reaching-students-emotional disturbances-lori-desautels

"Districts should appoint teacher-led teams to train staff about professional boundaries." (2006). *Educator's Guide to Controlling Sexual Harassment, 14*(2): 25.

Doidge, N. (2016). The brain's way of healing: *Remarkable discoveries and recoveries from the frontiers of neuroplasticity.* Penguin Books.

EMDR Institute. (n.d.). *What is EMDR?* Retrieved May 24, 2021 from, https://www.emdr.com/what-is-emdr/

Estes, R. J., Weiner, N. A. (2001). *The commercial sexual exploitation of children in the US, Canada and Mexico.* Philadelphia, PA: University of Pennsylvania, School of Social Work, Center for the Study of Youth Policy.

European Parliament. (2015, March 11). *Resolution of 11 March 2015 on child sexual abuse online.* Retrieved November 8, 2021 from, https://www.europarl.europa.eu/doceo/document/TA-8-2015-0070_EN.html

FBI National Press Office, (2020, March 23). *School closings due to COVID-19 present potential for increased risk of child exploitation* [Press Release]. https://www.fbi.gov news/pressrel/press-releases/school-closings-due-to-covid-19-present potential-for-increased-risk-of-child-exploitation

FBCH + One More Child. (2018, September 24). *One more child anti-trafficking overview* [Video File]. Retrieved May 20, 2021 from, https://vimeo.com/291571128

Florida Department for Education. (n.d.). *Child human trafficking.* Retrieved May 29, 2021 From, https://www.fldoe.org/core/fileparse.php/5411/urlt/HumanTraffickingToolkit.pdf

Forget, J. (2021, January 28). *Violent drug organization use human trafficking to expand profits.* U.S. Drug Enforcement Administration. https://www.dea.gov/stories/2021/2021-01/2021-01-28/violent-drug-organizations-use-human-trafficking-expand-profits

Frank, BrieAnna J. (2018, March 24). *Expert: 5 ways to help spot teacher sexual misconduct.* The Republic. https://www.azcentral.com/story/news local/arizona-education/2018/03/24/expert-5-ways-help-spot-teacher-sexual-misconduct/456283002/

Gillihan. S. J. (2016). *Retrain your brain (Cognitive behavioral therapy in 7 weeks: A workbook for managing depression and anxiety.* Althea Press.

Gillihan. S. J. (2018). *Cognitive behavioral therapy made simple: 10 strategies for managing anxiety, depression, anger, panic, and worry.* Althea Press.

Goldstein, Clark. (n.d.). *What to do (and not do) when children are anxious.* Child Mind Institute. Retrieved July 1, 2021 from, https://childmind.org/article/what-to-do-and-not-do-when-children-are-anxious/

Gordon, L. (2011). *Child welfare: A brief history.* Social Welfare History Project. http://socialwelfare.library.vcu.edu/programs/child-welfare-overview/

Griffin, Y. (2019). *In the hands of an abuser.* Xlibris.

Hagan, E. (2019, October 23). *When trauma gets stuck in the body.* Psychology Today. https://www.psychologytoday.com/us/blog/in-the-body/201910/when-trauma-gets-stuck-in-the-body

Harris, N. B. (2014, September). *How childhood trauma affects health across a lifetime* [Video File]. Retrieved May 24, 2021 from, https://www.ted.com/talks/nadine_burke_harris_how_childhood_trauma_affects_health_across_a_lifetime?language- en

Harvard Graduate School of Education. (2020). *Understanding the toll of toxic stress.* https://www.gse.harvard.edu/hgse100/story/understanding-toll-toxic-stress

Herman, J. L. (2015). *Trauma and recovery: The aftermath of violence—from domestic abuse to political terror.* Basic Books.

Hopper, J. (2018, April 3). *Freezing during sexual assault and harassment.* Psychology Today. https://www.psychologytoday.com/intl/blog/sexual-assault-and-thebrain/201804/freezing-during-sexual-assault-and-harassment

Huffington, A. (2016). *The sleep revolution: transforming your life, one night at a time.* Harmony Books.

International Centre for Missing and Exploited Children. (n.d.). *Glossary of Terms.* Retrieved November 11, 2021 from, https://www.icmec.org/resources/glossary/

Internet Safety 101. (n.d.) *Acronyms parents should know.* Retrieved July 6, 2021 from, https://internetsafety101.org/acronyms

Interpol. (n.d.). *Types of human trafficking.* Retrieved May 24, 2021 from, https://www.interpol.int/en/Crimes/Human-trafficking/Types-of-human-trafficking

Ivie, C. (2020, February). *How to talk with your kids about sex trafficking and exploitation Southwest Florida parent and child,* 56-57.

Jensen, C.J. (2019, May 31). "Sex Offenders 101": *Rapists, child molesters, and other sex offenders.* Idaho Council on Domestic Violence and Victim Assistance 2019 Conference Handouts. https://icdv.idaho.gov/wp-content/uploads/sites/80/2019/10/2019_Sex_Offenders_101.pdf

Juneau, A., Banta, A. (2018, September 18). *Human trafficking: What your campus needs to know* [Webinar]. National Center for Campus Public Safety. https://www.nccpsafety.org/training-technical-assistance/webinars/human-trafficking-what-your-campus-needs-to-know#embeds

Kentuckyslone. (2019, December 11). *The six leading causes of death can be attributed to stress.* HubPages. https://discover.hubpages.com/health/The-Six-Leading-Causes-of-Death-Can-Be-Attributed-to-Stress

Kimble, C. (2018, October 4). *Sexual assault remains dramatically underreported.* Brennan Center for Justice. https://www.brennancenter.org/our-work/analysis-opinion/sexual-assault-remains-dramatically-underreported

Knox, S. (2020, January 30). *Identifying and supporting students affected by human trafficking* [Webinar]. U.S. Department of Education. https:/safesupportivelearning.ed.gov/sites/default/files/HT%20Webinar_Jan%2030_Transcript%20FINAL.pdf

Lederer, L. J., & Wetzel, C. A. (2014). The health consequences of sex trafficking and their implications for identifying victims in healthcare facilities. *Annals of Health Law, 23*(1), 61-91.

Leyba, Erin. (2019, March 24). *10 better ways to help an anxious child calm down.* Psychology Today. https://www.psychologytoday.com/us/blog/joyful-parenting/201903/10-better-ways-help-anxious-child-calm-down

Litam, S. D. A. (2017). Human Sex Trafficking in America: What Counselors Need to Know. *Professional Counselor, 7*(1), 45-61.

Maryland Coalition Against Sexual Assault. (2016). *Behaviors of sexual predators: Grooming.* https://www.icmec.org/wp-content/uploads/2016/05/Behaviors-of-Sexual-Predators-Grooming.pdf

Mason, S. (2018, February 7). *Human trafficking: How hospitals can identify victims.* Vizient. https://newsroom.vizientinc.com/human-trafficking-how-hospitals-can-identify-victims.htm

Matar, M. Y. (2006). *Comprehensive legal approaches to combating trafficking in persons: An international and comparative perspective.* John Hopkins University. Paul H. Nitze School of Advanced International Studies. Protection Project. Retrieved November 8, 2021 from https://www.icmec.org/wp-content/uploads/2015/10/The_Protection_Project_Comprehensive_Approaches_to_THB.pdf

McGuire, M., & Dowling, S. (2013). Cyber-crime: A review of the evidence research report 75. Chapter 3: Cyber-enabled crimes- sexual offending against children. *Home Office*, 1-27, here 12. Retrieved November 8, 2021 from, https://www.gov.uk/government/uploads/system/uploads/attachment_data/file/246754/horr75-chap3.pdf

McKnight, P. (2006). Male prostitutes face enormous risks. *Prostitution and sex trafficking*, 57-6.

Minahan, Jessica. (2019, October, 1). *Trauma-informed teaching strategies*. ASCD. https://www.ascd.org/el/articles/trauma-informed-teaching-strategies

Muscara, C. (2019). *Stop missing your life: How to be deeply present in an un present world*. Hachette Books.

National Association of School Nurses. (2018). *The school nurse's role in behavioral mental health of students* [Position Statement]. https://higherlogicdownload.s3.amazonaws.com/NASN/3870c72d-fff9-4ed7-833f-215de278d256/UploadedImages/PDFs/Position%20Statements/2018-ps-behavioral-health.pdf

National Center for Missing & Exploited Children. (n.d.). *By the numbers*. Retrieved May 24, 2021 from, https://www.missingkids.org/gethelpnow/cybertipline#bythenumbers

National Center for Missing & Exploited Children. (n.d.). *The issues: Nonfamily abductions & attempts*. Retrieved May 24, 2021 from, https://www.missingkids.org/theissues/nonfamily

National Center for Missing & Exploited Children. (2019). *2019 reports by electronic service providers (ESP)*. https://www.missingkids.org/content/dam/missingkids/gethelp/2019-reports-by-esp.pdf

National Center for Victims of Crime. (n.d.). *Child sexual abuse statistics.* Retrieved May 20, 2021 from, https://victimsofcrime.org/child-sexual-abuse-statistics/

National Child Traumatic Stress Network. (n.d.) *School personnel.* Retrieved November 19, 2021 from, https://www.nctsn.org/audiences/school-personnel

National Child Traumatic Stress Network. (2003). *What is child traumatic stress?* https://www.nctsn.org/sites/default/files/resources//what_is_child_traumatic_stress.pdf

National Child Traumatic Stress Network. (2012, April). *Cognitive behavioral intervention for trauma in schools.* https://www.nctsn.org/sites/default/files/interventions/cbits_fact_sheet.pdf

National Institute of Mental Health. (2019, May). *Post-traumatic stress disorder.* https://www.nimh.nih.gov/health/topics/post-traumatic-stress-disorder-ptsd/

National Institute of Mental Health. (2020). *Post-traumatic stress disorder.* https://www.nimh.nih.gov/health/publications/post-traumatic-stress-disorder-ptsd/20-mh-8124-ptsd_38054.pdf

Niethammer, C. (2020, February 2). *Cracking the $150 billion business of human trafficking.* Forbes. https://www.forbes.com/sites/carmenniethammer/2020/02/02/cracking-the-150-billion-business-of-human-trafficking/?sh- 577ff4304142

Nixon, K., Tutty, L., Downe, P., Gorkoff, K., & Ursel, J. (2002). The everyday occurrence: Violence in the lives of girls exploited through prostitution. *Violence Against Women, 8*(9), 1016-1043.

Norton-Hawk, M. (2002). The lifecourse of prostitution. *Women, Girls & Criminal Justice*, 3(1), 7-9.

NPR. (2016, September 3). *School Nurses can be mental health 'detectives' but they need help*. NPR. https://www.npr.org/sections/ed/2016/09/03/478835294/school-nurses-can-be-mental-health-detectives-but-they-need-help

O'Donnell, B. (2021, April 30). *COVID-19 and missing & exploited children*. National Center for Missing and Exploited Children. https://www.missingkids.org/blog/2020/covid-19-and-missing-and-exploited-children

Owen, T. (2019, November 13). *NCMEC received over 18 million tips on exploitation of children in 2018*. NewsWest9. https://www.newswest9.com/article/news/crime/national-center-for-missing-exploited-children-over-18-million-reports-cyber-tipline/513-5fb13600-1423-438b-840a-3a735fe5beb0

Oxford University Press. (2013, July 24). *Brain research shows psychopathic criminals do not lack empathy, but fail to use it automatically. ScienceDaily*. www.sciencedaily.com/releases/2013/07/130724200412.htm

Palmieri, J., & Valentine, J. L. (2021). Using trauma-informed care to address sexual assault and intimate partner violence in primary care. *The Journal for Nurse Practitioners*, *17*(1), 44-48. https://doi.org/10.1016/j.nurpra.2020.08.028

Pandya, M., Altinay, M., Malone, D. A., & Anand, A. (2012). *Where in the brain is depression?*. Current Psychiatry Reports, 14(6), 634-642.

Parents Protect. (n.d.). *Warning signs in children and adults*. Stop It Now UK and Ireland. Retrieved May 24, 2021 from, https://www.parentsprotect.co.uk/warning-signs-in-children-and-adults.htm#WARNING%20SIGNS%20IN%20CHILDREN

Pemberton, J. V., & Loeb, T. B. (2020). Impact of Sexual and Interpersonal Violence and Trauma on Women: Trauma-Informed Practice and Feminist Theory. *Journal of Feminist Family Therapy, 32*(1-2), 115-131. https://doi.org/10.10 80/08952833.2020.1793564

Pennsylvania Coalition Against Rape. (n.d.). *What sex offenders were looking for in a child.* Retrieved May 24, 2021 from, https://pcar.org/what-sex-offenders-were-looking-for

Perina, J. (2017, January 18). *The brain can work against abuse victims.* Psychology Today. https://www.psychologytoday.com/us/blog/neurosagacity/201701/the-brain-can-work-against-abuse-victims

Philosophy Now. (n.d.). *How are the mind and brain related?* Retrieved May 24, 2021 from, https://philosophynow.org/issues/65/How_Are_The_Mind_And_Brain_Related

Polaris. (n.d). *Sex trafficking and LGBTQ youth.* Retrieved August 5, 2021 from https://polarisproject.org/wp-content/uploads/2019/09/LGBTQ-Sex-Trafficking.pdf

Polaris Project. (n.d.). *Domestic sex trafficking: The criminal operations of the American pimp.* Retrieved August 5, 2021 from https://www.dcjs.virginia.gov/sites/dcjs.virginia.gov/files/publications/victims/domestic-sex-trafficking-criminal-operations-american-pimp.pdf

RAINN. (n.d.). *Statistics.* Rape, Abuse, and Incest National Network. Retrieved May 20, 2021 from, https://www.rainn.org/statistics

RAINN. (n.d.) *Children and teens: Statistics. Rape, Abuse, and Incest National Network.* Retrieved June 26, 2021 from, https://www.rainn.org/statistics/children-and-teens

Reid, J. A., Baglivio, M. T., Piquero, A. R., Greenwald, M. A., & Epps, N. (2017). Human trafficking of minors and childhood adversity in Florida. *American Journal of Public Health, 107*(2), 306-311. https://www.ncbi.nlm.nih.gov/pmc/articles/PMC5227932/

Robert Wood Johnson Foundation. (2013, May 12). *The truth about ACEs infographic.* https://www.rwjf.org/en/library/infographics/the-truth-about-aces.html

Rosenfeld, J. (2018, October 23). *School nurses: The first line of treatment for mental health.* OZY. https://www.ozy.com/the-new-and-the-next/school-nurses-the-first-line-of-treatment-for-mental-health/89854/

Rubin, D.C., Boals, A., Berntsen, D. (2008). Memory in posttraumatic stress disorder: Properties of voluntary and involuntary, traumatic and non-traumatic autobiographical memories in people with and without PTSD symptoms. *Journal of Experimental Psychology: General, 137*(4), 591-614. https://doi.org/10.1037/a0013165

Rizzuto, A.P. and Crosson-Tower, C. (2016). *Child sexual abuse: reporting guidelines.* National Association of Independent Schools. Retrieved November 8, 2021 from, https://www.icmec.org/wp-content/uploads/2016/05/ChildSexualAbuse_RizzutoBookExcerpt.pdf

Saar, M.S., Epstein, R., Rosenthal L., Vafa, Y. (n.d.). *The sexual abuse to prison pipeline: The girls' story.* Georgetown Law. https://www.law.georgetown.edu/poverty-inequality-center/wp-content/uploads/sites/14/2019/02/The-Sexual-Abuse-To-Prison-Pipeline-The-Girls%E2%80%99-Story.pdf

San Diego County Office of Education. (n.d.) *Commercial sexual exploitation of children (CSEC) recommended protocols for schools.* Retrieved November 19, 2021 from, https://safesupportivelearning.ed.gov/resources/commercial-sexual-exploitation-children-csec-recommended-protocols-schools

Sanders, J. (2017, January 27). *12 confronting child sexual abuse statistics all parents need to know.* HuffPost. https://www.huffpost.com/entry/12-confronting-statistics-on-child-sexual-abuse_b_587dab01e4b0740488c3de49

Schimelpfening, N. (2021, May 6). *What is dialectical behavior therapy (DBT)?* Verywell Mind. https://www.verywellmind.com/dialectical-behavior-therapy-1067402

Schneider, M. B., Friedman, S. B., & Fisher, M. (1995). Stated and unstated reasons for visiting a high school nurse's office. *Journal of Adolescent Health, 16*(1), 35-40.

Senesac, S. (2021, February 24). *Florida ranked as one of the worst states for human trafficking.* Spinnaker. https://unfspinnaker.com/90192/news/florida-ranked-as-one-of-the-worst-states-for-human-trafficking/

Shakeshaft, C. (2004). *Educator sexual misconduct: A synthesis of existing literature.* U.S. Department of Education. https://www2.ed.gov/rschstat/research/pubs/misconductreview/report.pdf

Sidran Institute. (2019). *What are traumatic memories?* https://www.sidran.org/wp-content/uploads/2019/04/What-Are-Traumatic-Memories.pdf

Simons, D. A. (2014). *Sex offender typologies.* Office of Justice Programs: Sex Offender Management Assessment and Planning Initiative. https://smart.ojp.gov/somapi/chapter-3-sex-offender-typologies

Singh, A. (2021, March 20). *How much sleep do we really need?* Sleep Foundation. https://www.sleepfoundation.org/how-sleep-works/how-much-sleep-do-we-really-need

Sleep Foundation. (2020, November 4). *Sleep deprivation.* https://www.sleepfoundation.org/sleep-deprivation

Sleep Foundation. (2021, January 8). *PTSD and sleep.*
https://www.sleepfoundation.org/mental-health/ptsd-and-sleep

Sleep Foundation. (2021, January 15). *Trauma and sleep.*
https://www.sleepfoundation.org/mental-health/trauma-and-sleep

Sources of Strength. (n.d.). *Discover sources of strength.* Retrieved May 24, 2021
from, https://sourcesofstrength.org/discover/

Starecheski, L. (2015, March 2). *Take the ACE quiz- And learn what it
does and doesn't mean.* NPR. https://www.npr.org/sections/health-
shots/2015/03/02/387007941/take-the-ace-quiz-and-learn-what-it-does-
and-doesnt-mean

Stop It Now. (2008). *Prevent child sexual abuse: Facts about sexual abuse and how to
prevent it.* https://www.stopitnow.org/sites/default/files/documents/files/
prevent_child_sexual_abuse.pdf

Stop Street Harassment. (2018, February). *The facts behind the #metoo movement:
A national study on sexual harassment and assault.* https://www.nsvrc.
org/sites/default/files/2021-04/full-report-2018-national-study-on-sexual-
harassment-and-assault.pdf

Strosahl, K. D., & Robinson, P. J. (2015). *In this moment: Five steps to transcending
stress using mindfulness and neuroscience.* New Harbinger Publications.

Substance Abuse and Mental Health Services Administration (SAMHSA). (2014,
July). *SAMHSA's concept of trauma and guidance for a trauma-informed
approach.* SAMHSA's Trauma and Justice Strategic Initiative. https://
s3.amazonaws.com/static.nicic.gov/Library/028436.pdf

Substance Abuse and Mental Health Services Administration (SAMHSA). (2020). *Intimate partner violence and child abuse considerations during COVID-19.* https://www.samhsa.gov/sites/default/files/social-distancing-domestic-violence.pdf

Sutton, R. E. (2004). Emotional regulation goals and strategies of teachers. *Social psychology of education, 7*(4), 379-398. https://link.springer.com/article/10.1007/s11218-004-4229-y

Suzuki, E. (2017, November). *The brain-changing benefits of exercise* [Video File]. Retrieved May 24, 2021 from, https://www.ted.com/talks/wendy_suzuki_the_brain_changing_benefits_of_exercise

Teach Magazine. (n.d.). *How to engage disengaged students.* Retrieved July 1, 2021 from, https://teachmag.com/archives/4190

Thatcher, T. (2019, February 4). *Can emotional trauma cause brain damage?* Highland Springs. https://highlandspringsclinic.org/blog/can-emotional-trauma-cause-brain-damage/

The Life Coach. (n.d.). *What is the self coaching model?* Retrieved July 6, 2021 from, https://thelifecoachschool.com/self-coaching-model-guide/

Trauma and Learning Policy Initiative. (n.d.) *Traumatic experiences can impact learning, behavior and relationships at school.* Retrieved November 19, 2021 from, https://traumasensitiveschools.org/trauma-and-learning/the-problem-impact/

UNICEF USA. (2017, January 13). *What fuels human trafficking?* https://www.unicefusa.org/stories/what-fuels-human-trafficking/31692

UNICEF. (2020, December). *How many children and young people have internet access at home? Estimating digital connectivity during the COVID-19 pandemic.* https://data.unicef.org/resources/children-and-young-people-internet-access-at-home-during-covid19/

United Nation Human Rights Office of the High Commissioner. (2000, May 25). *Optional protocol to the convention on the rights of the child on the sale of children, child prostitution and child pornography. Article 2*. Retrieved November 8, 2021 from, https://www.ohchr.org/en/professionalinterest/pages/opsccrc.aspx

University of Northern Colorado. (2020, March 19). *Neurobiology of trauma*. Assault Survivors Advocacy Program. https://www.unco.edu/assault-survivors-advocacy-program/learn_more/neurobiology_of_trauma.aspx

University of Washington. (2017). *How to reduce stress through mindfulness* [Factsheet]. Healthy Aging & Physical Disability Rehabilitation Research Training Center, http://agerrtc.washington.edu

U.S. Department of Agriculture. (n.d.). *What's on your plate?* Retrieved May 24, 2021 from, https://www.myplate.gov/

U.S. Department of Health & Human Services, Administration for Children and Families, Administration on Children, Youth and Families, Children's Bureau. (2020). *Child Maltreatment 2018*. https://www.acf.hhs.gov/sites/default/files/documents/cb/cm2018.pdf

U.S. Department of Justice. (1997, February). *Sex offenses and offenders: an analysis of data on rape and sexual assault*. https://www.bjs.gov/content/pub/pdf/SOO.PDF

U.S. Department of State. (2007, August 8). *Health consequences of trafficking in persons* [Fact Sheet]. Office to Monitor and Combat Trafficking in Persons. https://2001-2009.state.gov/g/tip/rls/fs/07/91418.htm

U.S. Department of Veterans Affairs. (2019, October 16.). *How common is PTSD in women?* https://www.ptsd.va.gov/understand/common/common_women.asp

U.S. Department of Veterans Affairs. (2020, June 8). *PTSD basics.* https://www.ptsd.va.gov/understand/what/ptsd_basics.asp

Virginia Commission on Youth. (2017). *Collection of evidence-based practices for children and adolescents with mental health treatment needs,* 222-241. vcoy.virginia.gov/documents/collection/Collection2017online.pdf

Vyas, N. (2020, September 24). *How much sleep do babies and kids need?* Sleep Foundation. https://www.sleepfoundation.org/children-and-sleep/how-much-sleep-do-kids-need

Welch, M., Haskins, R. (2020, April 30). *What COVID-19 means for America's child welfare system.* Brookings. https://www.brookings.edu/research/what-covid-19-means-for-americas-child-welfare-system/

West, Mary. (2021, July 28). *What is the fight, flight, or freeze response?* Medical news today. https://www.medicalnewstoday.com/articles/fight-flight-or-freeze-response

Wetmore, A. (2019). *An introduction to coping with post-traumatic stress* (2nd ed.). Robinson.

Widman, L., Olson, M. A., & Bolen, R. M. (2013). Self-reported sexual assault in convicted sex offenders and community men. *Journal of Interpersonal Violence, 28*(7), 1519-1536.

Wolters Kluwer Health. (2018, April 24). *More than 1 in 20 children and teens have anxiety or depression.* Science Daily. https://www.sciencedaily.com/releases/2018/04/180424184119.htm

Wyman, P. A., Brown, C. H., LoMurray, M., Schmeelk-Cone, K., Petrova, M., Yu, Q., Walsh, E., Tu, X., & Wang, W. (2010). An outcome evaluation of the Sources of Strength suicide prevention program delivered by adolescent peer leaders in high schools. *American Journal of Public Health, 100*(9), 1653-1661.

YWCA. (2017, September). *Child sexual abuse facts.* https://www.ywca.org/wp-content/uploads/WWV-CSA-Fact-Sheet-Final.pdf